DOMINICAN REPUBLIC

Erin Foley & Leslie Jermyn

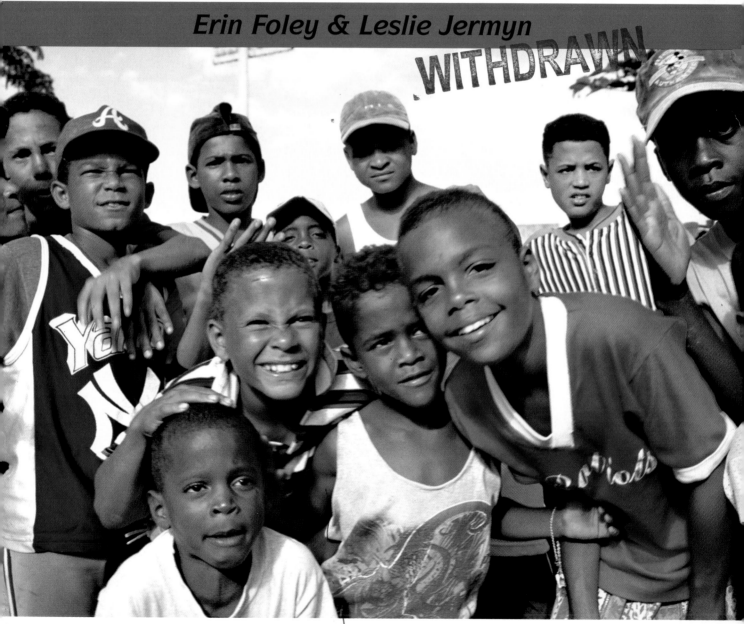

MARSHALL CAVENDISH BENCHMARK

NEW YORK

PICTURE CREDITS
Cover photo: © Getty Images: Angelo Cavalli
Bes Stock: 50, 114, 120 • Bettman Archive: 24, 25 • Buddy Mays Photography: 1, 30, 106 • Camera
Press: 26, 28 • Douglas Donne Bryant Stock Photography: 15, 18, 21, 31, 34, 36, 41, 46, 47, 61, 76,
100, 102, 103 (top), 104, 117, 118, 128 • Dave G. Houser/Houserstock: 5 • Hulton-Deutsch: 17, 75
• Hutchison Library: 6, 51, 52, 53, 14, 29, 39, 40, 42, 43, 44, 45, 58, 60, 62, 64, 66, 68, 69, 74, 78,
84, 95, 103 (bottom), 108, 121, 123, 126, 129 • The Image Bank: 10, 12 • James Davis Worldwide:
48, 82 • Björn Klingwall: 20, 69, 78, 84 • Life File Photo Library: 3, 9, 11, 16, 23, 35, 59, 63, 70, 71,
79, 80, 81, 93, 96, 97, 107, 109, 112, 113, 119, 122, 124, 125 • Lonely Planet Images: 38, 54, 56, 90
• Panos Pictures: 8 • Reuters: 33, 49 • David Simson: 4, 7, 13, 57, 67, 72, 73, 89, 101, 111 • Studio
Bonisolli/Stockfood: 131 • Times Editions: 130

PRECEDING PAGE
A group of young baseball players at a park in the Dominican capital, Santo Domingo.

Marshall Cavendish Benchmark
99 White Plains Road
Tarrytown, NY 10591
Website: www.marshallcavendish.us

Originated and designed by Times Editions
An imprint of Marshall Cavendish International (Asia) Private Limited
A member of Times Publishing Limited

Library of Congress Cataloging-in-Publication Data
Foley, Erin, 1967-
    Dominican Republic / by Erin Foley. – 2nd ed.
      p. cm. – (Cultures of the world)
    Summary: "Explores the geography, history, government, economy, people,
      and culture of the Dominican Republic" – Provided by publisher.
    Includes bibliographical references and index.
    ISBN 0-7614-1966-7
    1. Dominican Republic – Juvenile literature. I. Title. II. Series.
    F1934.2.F65 2005
    972.93 — dc22   2005009361

Printed in China

7 6 5 4 3 2 1

CONTENTS

Many rural Dominicans leave for the cities in the hope of finding a better life.

A dancer shows off the bright colors of a traditional costume, and the cheerful friendliness of Dominicans.

INTRODUCTION

THE DOMINICAN REPUBLIC shares the Caribbean island of Hispaniola with Haiti. The Dominican capital city, Santo Domingo, was established more than 500 years ago, the first European colony in the Western Hemisphere. European diseases and abuses virtually wiped out the indigenous people. Most Dominicans today are of mixed ancestry, tracing their roots to the European colonists and African slaves.

Economically and politically, the Dominican Republic has moved away from a reliance on sugar, and the sugar elite's dictatorial authority, to new agricultural and industrial sectors of the economy, and regular, orderly elections. In the 21st century, Dominicans face the challenge of healing deep social divisions caused by racism and the uneven distribution of wealth in their country. At the same time, they enjoy a culture that is rich in artistic tradition and a landscape that is blessed with natural beauty.

GEOGRAPHY

THE DOMINICAN REPUBLIC occupies central and eastern Hispaniola, the second-largest island, after Cuba, in the West Indies. Hispaniola is located between Cuba to the northwest and Puerto Rico to the east. The western third of Hispaniola is occupied by the country of Haiti.

The Dominican Republic has an area of 18,680 square miles (48,380 square km) and a 800-mile (1,288-km) coastline, washed by the Atlantic Ocean to the north and the Caribbean Sea to the south.

With the widest variation in elevation in the West Indies, the island of the Dominican Republic has great geographical diversity concentrated in a small area. The country's terrain includes mountain ranges, semidesert lowlands, fertile valleys, tropical rain forests, picturesque beaches, rivers, and even a saltwater lake.

Left: **Beef cattle are raised on medium- to large-size ranches in the eastern Dominican Republic.**

Opposite: **The green coast near Puerto Plata.**

REGIONS

Four mountain ranges divide the Dominican Republic into northern, central, and southwestern regions. The main range is the Cordillera Central, which forms the backbone of the country, with smaller, but nonetheless impressive, mountain ranges on either side.

NORTHERN REGION The Dominican Republic's Atlantic coastal plain extends between the cities of Monte Cristi and Nagua. The Cordillera Septentrional, the range farthest north, rises from this plain in moderate peaks around 3,280 feet (1,000 m) high.

The scenic mountains near Constanza, in the fertile central region.

Banana plantations cover a valley.

The densely populated farmland of the Cibao Valley lies south of the Cordillera Septentrional. The country's second-largest city, Santiago, is located in the valley and is its commercial center. East of Santiago, the valley is called the Vega Real, or Royal Plain, where the land is fertile and suitable for the cultivation of crops such as coffee, corn, and tobacco.

CENTRAL REGION The Cordillera Central dominates the midsection of the Dominican Republic. This mountain range starts west of the capital city, Santo Domingo, and rises northwest to the Haitian border. The Cordillera Central contains the highest point in the West Indies—Pico Duarte, at 10,417 feet (3,175 m). In the eastern coastal plain, limestone terraces rise almost 400 feet (122 m) near the foothills of the Cordillera Oriental. In the western edge of the region lies the San Juan Basin.

SOUTHWESTERN REGION Here, the Sierra de Neiba towers over the Hoya de Enriquillo, a bare and dusty valley containing the largest lake in the Caribbean islands. Lake Enriquillo, once part of a strait, is filled with saltwater and lies 150 feet (46 m) below sea level. Crocodiles live in the lake, and flamingos can be found nearby.

9

RIVERS

The Yaque del Norte is the longest river in the Dominican Republic, its flow broken only by the Tavera Dam. The river flows through the northern slopes of the Cordillera Central, waters agricultural land in the Cibao Valley, and then forms a delta on the northern coast as it empties into the Atlantic Ocean.

In the south, the Yaque del Sur is the most important river. Flowing through the southern slopes of the Cordillera Central, this river waters the San Juan and Hoya de Enriquillo basins and empties into Neiba Bay on the southern coast, through a delta.

Lake Enriquillo, in the southwest, is the focus of a drainage basin that exceeds 1,158 square miles (3,000 square km) in area, including 102 square miles (265 square km) covered by the salty lake. The basin includes 10 minor river systems. The northern rivers flow year-round in the Sierra de Neiba; the southern rivers rise in the Sierra de Bahoruco only after heavy rainfall.

Other rivers include the Yuna, which waters the Vega Real and empties into the Bay of Samaná; the Ozama, which irrigates the Caribbean plain and enters the sea near Santo Domingo; and the Artibonite, which flows west from the Cordillera Central through Haiti to the Golfe de la Gonâve.

CLIMATE

Trade winds and high elevations moderate the Dominican Republic's tropical climate. The average annual temperature hovers around 77°F (25°C), with temperatures ranging from 69°F (21°C) in high mountain areas to 82°F (28°C) in coastal areas.

There are two seasons: rainy from May to November and dry the rest of the year. Moist trade winds from the Atlantic Ocean bring the most rain to the northeast of the country—100 inches (2,540 mm) per year, on average. As they blow across the country, the winds dry out, leaving areas near the Haitian border with little rain—30 inches (760 mm) per year, on average. Periodic droughts ruin crops and cause severe water shortages, while annual floods occur in areas where drainage is poor.

Hurricanes are an occasional threat. The storms develop during September in the Atlantic Ocean or in the Caribbean Sea. The most destructive hurricanes have killed hundreds of people and caused extensive loss of property. In 1930 a hurricane killed about 8,000 people in the country and, in 1998, the Dominican Republic was the worst-hit Caribbean nation in the path of Hurricane Georges.

Above: **Trade winds and sea breezes keep coastal homes relatively cool.**

Opposite: **Palm trees grace river banks near Santo Domingo.**

Flora in the eastern mountainous region includes ferns, lianas, bromeliads, and orchids.

FLORA

With a diverse geography, the Dominican Republic is home to a variety of plant species, many of them native to Hispaniola. These include the ceiba (silk-cotton) tree, one of the biggest trees in the Central American tropical forest. The indigenous people made practical use of ceiba, crafting canoes from its wood, but the tree also had a spiritual significance for them; it represented the link between heaven and earth.

Plants that these early settlers cultivated are still common in the Dominican Republic today. These include manioc, several kinds of pepper, papaya, tobacco, and *higuero* (ee-GOOAIR-oh), or calabash tree, which they used to make ceremonial masks and eating utensils.

The humid mountain forests in the east support the most lush vegetation. Mahogany trees thrive in abundance; their hard wood was used to build the altar of Santa María la Menor in Santo Domingo, the first cathedral in the Americas.

The higher mountain forests in the Cordillera Central are made up of conifers such as the Creolean pine. Cactus and agave characterize the desert and semiarid areas of the southwest. The coastal flora include mangroves and palms, such as the coconut palm, which was imported from Africa, and the native royal palm.

The Spanish settlers introduced food crops such as cocoa, coffee, mangoes, bananas, and sugarcane, and trees such as the African tulip tree and the poinciana, also known as the flamboyant tree.

FAUNA

One of the most unusual animals in the Dominican Republic is the solenodon. It looks like a rat with an anteater's snout. Another rodent found in the country is the hutia, which looks like a rabbit with short ears and a long tail. Both animals are endangered.

Other mammals include the West Indian manatee and the bottle-nose dolphin. Humpback whales live in the Bay of Samaná from December through March. The Spanish settlers brought cows, pigs, donkeys, horses, cats, and rats. The mongoose, imported from India, is now a pest in the Dominican Republic.

Reptiles, especially frogs, snakes, and lizards, are abundant in the country. Tree frogs live on palm trees and even on telephone poles. The American crocodile, rhinoceros iguana, and Ricords iguana are endangered. Scorpions inhabit the drier areas, finding shade under rocks. Spiders are numerous, including tarantulas, but usually not poisonous.

Birds sighted in the Dominican Republic include mockingbirds, thrashers, woodpeckers, and the rare perico parakeet and Hispaniolan parrot. Fish include grouper, barracuda, parrotfish, leatherjacket, sawfish, Spanish and frigate mackerel, red snapper, mullet, sardines, and eels. The beaches and tidepools yield a variety of crabs and snails. Anthozoa produce calcium carbonate, which forms much of the island's surface, as well as abundant coral reefs on the northwestern coast and parts of the southern coast.

The birds of the Dominican Republic include flamingos.

Dense settlement in Santo Domingo.

CITIES

SANTO DOMINGO The first city founded by Europeans in the Americas, Santo Domingo has many of the region's oldest buildings, such as the first cathedral (Santa María la Menor) and university (Autonomous University of Santo Domingo). Other colonial structures include the Castle of Colón and the Tower of Homage. Restored in the 1970s, the old city preserves its cobblestone streets, outdoor markets, and small craftsmen's shops. Santo Domingo remains the cultural center of the Dominican Republic.

Santo Domingo is the capital, the seat of the national government, and the economic center of the country. The city has a population of more than 2 million. It attracts the majority of the migrants from the countryside and small towns, and construction rushes to keep up with the influx. Many migrants live in slums in and around the city. Santo Domingo is also home to the suburbs and supermarkets of most of the country's growing middle class.

SANTIAGO DE LOS CABALLEROS With a population of 824,607, Santiago is the Dominican Republic's second-largest city. Besides being the country's agricultural center, Santiago is also a city of refinement that takes pride in its long tradition of aristocratic families.

14

LA ROMANA Located on the southern coast, La Romana is a relaxed provincial capital. Traditionally the center of the sugar industry, it is also a popular resort area.

La Romana was long considered a company town. In the 1970s the U.S.-based multinational corporation Gulf-Western was one of the largest property owners in the Dominican Republic. The company invested heavily in sugar, cattle, tourism, cement, and real estate. Critics say that the company often employed administrators who bribed local politicians, police officers, and military commanders.

To show goodwill, Gulf-Western built schools, churches, clinics, employee housing, recreation centers, and the famous Casa de Campo resort in La Romana. The company sold its holdings in the 1980s, but La Romana continues to maintain and develop the initial infrastructure.

PUERTO PLATA Located north of Santiago at the foot of Mount Isabel de Torres, Puerto Plata (Silver Port) was founded in 1503 by Christopher Columbus. This scenic city is the center of the Dominican Republic's hotel and resort industry and competes with the capital as the island's top tourist destination. West of Puerto Plata lie the ruins of La Isabela, which Columbus founded in 1493.

The rapid growth of Puerto Plata, along with investment by European and North American companies, stimulates tourism development in surrounding towns.

HISTORY

DOMINICAN HISTORY IS FULL of dramatic power struggles. The country has been shaped by its most authoritarian rulers, who are often admired for their strength and for the order and stability they imposed, despite their brutality and abuses of power.

Dominicans had to fight for their independence several times. Throughout its history, the Dominican Republic has been subject to the influence of outside powers. It has come under the rule of two European colonial powers, Spain and France, as well as its neighbors Haiti and the United States.

PRE-COLUMBIAN HISPANIOLA

When Christopher Columbus (in Spanish, Cristóbal Colón) landed on the island of Hispaniola, he met a friendly and peaceful people who called themselves Taino, a name meaning good or noble, to distinguish themselves from their warlike Carib neighbors, who were rumored to be cannibals. The Taino were members of the Arawak family, the indigenous people of the Greater Antilles and South America.

The Taino Arawak who greeted Columbus lived in large, permanent settlements and wore jewelry, some made from gold. Columbus called them Indians, thinking that he had reached the far eastern edge of Asia.

Scholars estimate that the population of Hispaniola numbered about 500,000 during the time of the Spanish arrival. Taino Arawak culture had spread throughout much of the Antilles, but the Taino Arawak of Hispaniola and Puerto Rico were the most populous and most culturally complex. The Taino Arawak had no written language.

Above: **Christopher Columbus reached Hispaniola in 1492.**

Opposite: **The Panteón Nacional, established in 1747 as a Jesuit monastery, houses the remains of prominent 19th-century Spaniards, including General Pedro Santana, who arranged the annexation of the Dominican Republic by Spain in 1861.**

AGRICULTURE The Taino Arawak developed a system of agriculture in which they formed mounds of earth into raised beds called *conuco* (koh-NOO-koh). On these beds they planted crops such as corn, sweet potatoes, and most importantly manioc, which was used to make flour for bread. They also cultivated squash, beans, peppers, and peanuts, which were boiled with meat or fish. Around their homes the Taino Arawak planted fruit, calabashes, cotton, and tobacco for cigars. Europeans first learned of tobacco in the Caribbean.

A Taino Arawak artifact carved in wood.

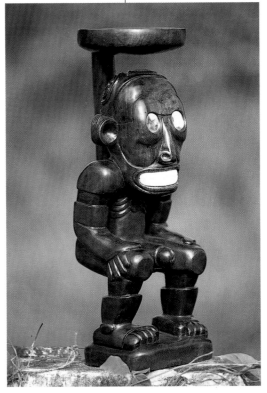

RELIGION The Taino Arawak worshiped deities called *zemis* (SAY-mees), a word that also referred to the idols and fetishes they carried. The supreme deities were Yúcahu, the god of manioc and the sea, and his mother, Atabey, the goddess of fertility and fresh water. Lesser deities included spirits in trees, rocks, and other parts of the landscape, and the spirits of ancestors, who held great importance.

HOME AND TRAVEL The Taino Arawak lived in homes made from wood and thatch, in villages of 1,000 to 2,000 people. Each village was ruled by a cacique, who could be a man or a woman.

The villages were organized into district chiefdoms, which were then organized into five regional chiefdoms. The Taino Arawak made sea voyages on trade routes. They traveled in canoes made from ceiba wood; their large canoes could carry up to 150 people.

WHERE THE TAINO ARAWAK CAME FROM

The Taino Arawak believed their ancestors came from caves in a sacred mountain on Hispaniola. Anthropologists say they were descendants of two races originating in Mesoamerica and South America. Hispaniola was originally settled around 4000 B.C. by a race of people who moved from Mesoamerica to the islands of Cuba and Hispaniola. These people were supplanted 4,600 years later by descendants of South American Arawak.

The Arawak migrated to the Antilles from the coast of South America sometime in the first millennium B.C., supplanting the original inhabitants of the Lesser Antilles, who had also come to the islands from South America, around 2000 B.C. During these centuries of occupation in the Lesser Antilles, Arawak culture changed and adapted. The Arawak finally succeeded in colonizing the eastern tip of Hispaniola around A.D. 200.

There they lived for another 400 years, and their culture continued to evolve. Around A.D. 600 they spread west across Hispaniola and into the interior. These migrants became the ancestors of the Taino Arawak whom Columbus encountered almost 900 years later.

"I assure Your Highness that I believe that in all the world there is no better people nor better country. They love their neighbors as themselves, and they have the sweetest talk in the world, and are gentle and always laughing."

—*Christopher Columbus, in 1492, describing the indigenous peoples he met during his travels*

Wood-and-thatch houses of the Taino Arawak.

SPANISH CONQUEST AND COLONIZATION

The promise of gold in Hispaniola attracted wealth-seeking adventurers from Spain. The Taino Arawak were forced to work as laborers in the gold and silver mines. The Spaniards used them mercilessly, forcing them to work long hours, stealing their supplies, demanding large amounts of tribute from them, and abusing the women. Some of the indigenous people committed suicide by hanging themselves or drinking poisonous manioc juice. Many more died from exposure to European diseases, for which they had no immunity. Although peaceful by nature, the Taino Arawak were driven to rebellion in 1495, but the Spaniards crushed the revolt. By 1524 the Taino Arawak had ceased to exist as a unified people.

The Castle of Colón was built in Santo Domingo in 1523 by Diego Colón, the son of Columbus.

FIRST PRIEST OF THE AMERICAS

Bartolomé de Las Casas (1474–1566) was the first priest to be ordained in America, and he was the main advocate for indigenous people in the Americas. He started out as an adventurer and a slave owner, but he soon became appalled by the inhumane treatment of the indigenous people and spoke out against the abuse they suffered at the hands of the colonists.

BARTOLOMÉ DE LAS CASAS

Las Casas spent the rest of his life pressuring the Spanish crown to protect the local people. In 1542 he convinced King Charles V to sign laws abolishing the *encomienda* system and requiring Spanish colonists to free their slaves. The writings of Las Casas, the first official to decry the injustice of colonial rule, lived on after the man, inspiring independence movements in later centuries.

"Who of those born in future centuries will believe this? I myself who am writing this and saw it and know most about it can hardly believe that such is possible."

—*Father Bartolomé de Las Casas, on the colonists' abusive treatment of the indigenous people*

In 1503 the colonists of Santo Domingo began to import slaves from Africa to meet the growing demand for labor in the cultivation of sugarcane. By 1520 the labor force of Santo Domingo consisted almost exclusively of African slaves.

The huge tracts of land originally granted by the Spanish crown gave the landowners virtually sovereign authority. The political culture of the caudillo, or military dictator, developed. The caudillos often had a magnetic personality that attracted the loyalty of the people.

By the early 16th century, Santo Domingo had begun to decline. The colony stagnated for the next 250 years, as the Spanish crown gave its attention to the richer territories of Mexico and Peru. In the 16th and 17th centuries, life in Santo Domingo was interrupted only occasionally by armed engagements with French and English pirates. In 1586 the English admiral Sir Francis Drake captured Santo Domingo, demanding a ransom from the Spanish government for its return.

SAINT DOMINGUE AND SANTO DOMINGO

Harassed by pirates, in 1697 Spain signed the Treaty of Ryswick, ceding the western third of Hispaniola to France. France named its new colony Saint Domingue, which developed into the most productive colony in the Americas and imported many slaves to drive its economy.

In 1791 the slaves of Saint Domingue rose up against their owners. A former slave, François-Dominique Toussaint L'Ouverture, formed an army to free the slaves. Initially, he joined the Spanish forces in their war against France. Later, he joined the French forces against the Spaniards. In 1795 Spain signed the Treaty of Basel, ceding Santo Domingo to France.

Toussaint's goal remained the freedom of his people. He conquered Santo Domingo in 1801 and reformed the government, but in 1802 the French commander Napoleon Bonaparte sent troops to take Toussaint to France. Toussaint died in prison there in 1803. France fought the revolutionaries in Hispaniola until 1808/1809, when Spain regained Santo Domingo.

In 1821 the Dominicans deposed the Spanish governor, José Nuñez de Cáceres, and declared Santo Domingo independent. They called the new nation Spanish Haiti. Before long, the Haitian president, Jean-Pierre Boyer, invaded Spanish Haiti. The Haitian occupation from 1821 to 1843 was marked by economic decline and created a deep resentment among the Dominicans toward the Haitians.

DUARTE—FATHER OF THE REPUBLIC

He never held the office of president, but Juan Pablo Duarte is known as the father of the Dominican Republic.

In 1833, after seven years of study in Europe, Duarte, the son of a prominent Santo Domingo family, returned home. Unlike the caudillo, he was principled, idealistic, ascetic in his habits, and a genuine nationalist. In 1838 he organized a secret resistance movement called La Trinitaria, or The Trinity.

Unfortunately, Duarte was sick and out of the country when the moment of revolution arrived in 1844. When he returned to the new Dominican Republic, the people welcomed him with great adulation and celebration. Within a year of independence, however, a caudillo, Pedro Santana, seized power and exiled Duarte, who spent the rest of his life in Venezuela, where he died in 1876.

INDEPENDENCE

Juan Pablo Duarte and a group of co-conspirators led a revolution that ended successfully on February 27, 1844, forming the Dominican Republic. The date is now celebrated as Independence Day.

For the next 20 years, General Pedro Santana Familias and General Buenaventura Báez Méndez fought for power and took turns seizing the presidency. Each used his position to enrich himself, his family, and his supporters at the public's expense.

Santana had the Dominican Republic annexed by Spain in 1861 to protect it from the Haitians. However, the Dominicans rebelled, and in 1865 the Queen of Spain repealed the annexation, prompted in part by the United States. The United States' attention was no longer consumed by the Civil War, and the United States wished to renew its enforcement of the Monroe Doctrine, which prohibited the presence of European powers in the Western Hemisphere.

After Spain's departure, a power struggle ensued between the southern region and the northern Cibao region. From 1865 until 1882, the presidency changed hands 12 times.

FROM DICTATORSHIP TO ANARCHY

The power struggles after the restoration in 1865 ended temporarily during the presidency of Ulises Heureaux in 1882. In spite of a constitutional two-year term limit, he managed to maintain power until his death in 1899. His personal extravagance and the support of his secret police resulted in a mounting foreign debt that weighed heavily on the economy. Heureaux was assassinated on July 26, 1899, passing through the town of Moca.

The country was plunged into renewed factionalism and economic disaster, as foreign governments called for repayment of the loans Heureaux had incurred. In 1905 the United States increased their interest in Caribbean affairs and signed a financial accord with the Dominican Republic, in which the United States took responsibility for repaying the Dominican Republic's debts by collecting all customs duties and allocating the revenues. This lasted until 1941.

Ulises Heureaux ruled the Dominican Republic from 1882 to 1899. He manipulated elections, repressed dissent, circulated destructive rumors about his political opponents, and attacked and imprisoned their supporters. He also established an extensive network of secret police, spies, and assassins.

Heated political rivalries continued to create violence and instability. U.S. president Woodrow Wilson finally sent in the U.S. Marines to establish control, and declared a military government in November 1916. The United States cited fears that Europe would try to intervene in the Dominican conflict, which would be a violation of the U.S.-proclaimed Monroe Doctrine.

The Marines restored order throughout most of the country, and economic growth resumed as the military government balanced the budget, reduced the debt, and improved the infrastructure. For the first time, all the regions were linked by roads. The United States replaced

the Dominican military with a professional force called the Dominican Constabulary Guard. Later in the century, this army would be used to repress civilians under dictatorial rule.

Despite the improvements, Dominicans resented the loss of their independence; nor was the U.S. occupation of the island particularly popular in the United States. On June 21, 1921, U.S. president Warren G. Harding proposed a plan for withdrawal. The final agreement included a few requirements: democratic elections, a loan from the United States of $2.5 million for public works and other expenses, and acceptance of U.S. officers in the National Guard. The U.S. occupation ended with the election of Horacio Vásquez Lajara on March 15, 1924.

The period immediately following the occupation experienced increased exports, expanded public works, and an improved economy. In 1927, however, Vásquez tried to extend his term from four to six years, providing the catalyst for struggles between rival caudillos.

The U.S. occupation of the Dominican Republic completed U.S. control of Hispaniola, since the United States had seized control of Haiti in 1915.

Trujillo's massacre of 20,000 Haitians living in the Dominican Republic and his attempt to assassinate the president of Venezuela turned international, and particularly U.S., opinion against him, and eventually led to his assassination.

ERA OF TRUJILLO

Factional rivalries were squelched with the election of General Rafael Leonidas Trujillo Molina in 1930. The army ensured his election by harassing and intimidating electoral officials and eliminating potential political opponents. At Trujillo's request, the "Era of Trujillo" was proclaimed by the congress at his inauguration.

Trujillo dominated Dominican politics for more than 30 years. He held office from 1930 to 1938, and again from 1942 to 1952, regardless of constitutional term limitations, and in the interim years, he ruled through puppet presidents. Many Dominicans contend that his influence is still alive today.

Under Trujillo, the quality of life improved for many Dominicans. The economy expanded, the foreign debt was eliminated, the currency remained stable, the middle class grew, and public-works projects proliferated. Trujillo improved the road system, expanded port facilities, and constructed airports and public buildings. He improved the system of public education, which decreased the illiteracy rate.

There was a dark side to his rule, however. He maintained a highly effective secret police force that monitored, and sometimes eliminated, opponents both at home and abroad. He maintained his base of support in the military by paying the officers well, giving them generous side benefits, expanding their forces and equipment, and controlling them through fear, patronage, and rotating assignments. He also used the state to enrich himself enormously; by the end of his rule, the Trujillo family was the largest landowner in the Dominican Republic. His most outrageous deed was the 1937 massacre of more than 20,000 Haitians living in the Dominican Republic, in retaliation for the Haitian government's execution of his most valued covert agents in Haiti.

Trujillo also became increasingly paranoid about his personal safety. At one point in 1960 he tried to assassinate the Venezuelan president, Rómulo Betancourt, fearing that Betancourt was plotting against him.

The Organization of American States called for an end to diplomatic relations with the Dominican Republic in 1960; the United States broke relations soon after. On May 30, 1961, Trujillo was assassinated with weapons provided by the U.S. Central Intelligence Agency.

TRUJILLO—CAUDILLO EXTRAORDINARIO

Rafael Leonidas Trujillo Molina was a product of the military constabulary created under the U.S. occupation. He was a commander who came from a humble background. He had enlisted in the National Police in 1918, when upper-class Dominicans were refusing to collaborate with the occupying forces of the United States.

Trujillo rose quickly in the officer corps, all the while building a network of allies and supporters. However much the U.S. officials wanted to see the new military as a professional and apolitical force, Trujillo knew that it was, in fact, the main source of power in the Republic, and that it would be his path to power.

He inspired both fear and awe in Dominicans. Because they desired peace and dreaded chaos, the Dominican people admired Trujillo for the order he imposed on society; but they feared the means by which he achieved this order. He is nostalgically remembered by many Dominicans as a stern father.

After being deposed by a coup in 1963, Bosch ran for president again in 1966. Balaguer won with 57 percent of the vote, partly because many Dominicans were afraid that voting for Bosch would incite renewed violence. Bosch never regained the presidency.

CIVIL WAR

After a few brief struggles for power, Dominicans elected Juan Bosch Gaviño as president on December 20, 1962, in the country's first free elections in nearly 40 years. Bosch was a scholar and poet who, while in exile, had organized opposition to Trujillo through the Dominican Revolutionary Party (PRD). His social and economic policies, such as land reform, demonstrated concern for the welfare of the poor.

The 1963 constitution separated church and state, guaranteed civil and individual rights, and endorsed civilian control of the military. Powerful institutions such as the military and the church resented these restrictions and warned that the constitution was influenced by Communists and that it would lead to "another Cuba." On September 25, 1963, the military staged a coup.

Bosch supporters and members of the PRD, calling themselves Constitutionalists (in reference to the 1963 constitution), launched a revolution on April 25, 1965. Conservative forces in the military, calling themselves Loyalists, retaliated the next day. The Constitutionalists refused to back down.

On April 28, the United States sent a force of 20,000 to Santo Domingo in support of the Loyalists, believing that the Constitutionalists were dominated by Communists. A provisional government was established, and elections were organized for July of the following year. Meanwhile, violent skirmishes continued.

DEMOCRACY AND GLOBAL ECONOMICS

The elections of 1966, between the deposed president, Juan Bosch, and Trujillo's designated successor, Joaquín Balaguer, introduced into Dominican politics a rivalry that would continue for decades. Balaguer served as president for 22 of the next 30 years. Support for his administration rose and fell with the ups and downs of the republic's sugar-dependent economy.

In 1978 Antonio Guzmán Fernández, the PRD candidate, won the presidency. He combined social and economic reforms with conservative fiscal measures to combat rising oil prices and falling sugar prices. Although his administration suffered from a declining economy and, in 1979, severe hurricane damage, his party retained the presidency in 1982, when Salvador Jorge Blanco was elected president. A recession in the United States and Europe and the Dominican Republic's foreign-debt crisis forced Blanco to implement rationing, which led to riots in 1985. Balaguer won back the presidency in 1986 and was reelected three times before Leonel Fernández Reyna defeated him in 1996. Balaguer died in 2002.

Leonel Fernández continued Balaguer's work by reducing barriers to trade and encouraging foreign investment through tourism and free-trade zones (FTZs). His first term saw rapid growth in both sectors. In 2000 Hipólito Mejía was elected president. Unfortunately, the economy slowed dramatically after the attacks on the World Trade Center in New York in 2001. High oil prices also limited growth. In 2003 the republic's banks suffered severe crises, and in the elections of 2004, voters rejected Mejía and returned Leonel Fernández to power for a second term.

Balaguer followed the dictator Trujillo's example in intimidating his opponents and controlling the military. Bosch's party, the PRD, boycotted the 1970 and 1974 elections in order to avoid attacks on its candidates. Also, like Trujillo, Balaguer used the National Police as a tool of repression.

GOVERNMENT

THE DOMINICAN REPUBLIC'S dramatic history is centered on politics. Political power almost always depends on who one knows—family, friends, and business associates. Formal organizations are important, but informal ties carry even greater weight.

The Dominican Republic wavers between two political traditions: authoritarianism and democracy. Dominicans admire the principles of a liberal democracy in the abstract, but they often privately prefer the disciplined rule of a strong caudillo. Many Dominicans seem to fear that democracy will not work in their country. Over the decades since the end of the Trujillo dictatorship, certain democratic principles have become accepted, but many only superficially so.

ELECTORAL SYSTEM

Voting is compulsory in the Dominican Republic for all citizens 18 years or older and for any married individuals regardless of age. The requirement is not enforced, however. Members of the police or armed forces are not allowed to vote, nor are imprisoned criminals. Ballots are color-coded to compensate for the high rate of illiteracy. Voters receive two separate ballots for each of the competing political parties. They deposit one for the presidential election and one for all other contested offices. This system, in effect, forces the voter to elect a party rather than an individual to office, thus explaining why the president's party almost always carries a majority in congress.

Opposite: **The National Palace in Santo Domingo, the Dominican capital.**

Below: **A carload of enthusiastic voters. The Dominican Republic's electoral system was established after Trujillo's assassination in 1961, at the recommendation of the Organization of American States.**

CONSTITUTION OF 1966

Emerging from the Trujillo era, Dominicans desired a firm commitment to constitutionalism, that is, loyalty to a set of governing principles rather than loyalty to a leader. The constitutionalist ideal was not popular with aspiring caudillo, but the constitution adopted on November 28, 1966 has lasted to the present, with reforms effected on July 25, 2002. The amendments passed in 2002 dealt with the nation's electoral system, including the reelection of the president.

The 1966 document formed a compromise between the authoritarian history of the Dominican Republic and the ideals of democracy. While it established a lengthy list of basic rights and civil liberties and provided for a strengthened legislature, it also granted a great deal of power to the president, including emergency measures that, whenever exercised, historically have preceded a slide into dictatorship.

The 1966 constitution reaffirmed and strengthened several basic democratic principles that traditionally had been present in the Dominican Republic, but not always exercised. These basic principles included representative government by direct vote; the separation of powers into executive, legislative, and judicial branches; a system of checks and balances between the branches of government; and the right to civil and political liberties.

EXECUTIVE POWER

The president and the vice-president of the Dominican Republic are directly elected. They are limited to a four-year term but may run for reelection. The president appoints a cabinet of around 20 department heads and, as executive, has authority over the appointment and dismissal of almost all public officials.

The Dominican Republic has a strong executive office. The 1966 constitution gives the president the power to promulgate laws passed by congress; to engage in diplomatic relations; and to command, deploy, and make appointments in the armed forces. His extensive emergency powers include the authority to suspend basic rights in times of emergency, to postpone congressional sessions, to declare a state of siege, and to rule by decree.

PRESIDENT LEONEL FERNÁNDEZ REYNA

Leonel Fernández Reyna was born in 1953 in the Dominican Republic. He grew up in New York but returned to his homeland to attend the Autonomous University in Santo Domingo, where he attained a doctorate in law in 1978. Since his university days, he has been active in Dominican politics.

In the presidential elections of 1990, Fernández ran as running mate to Juan Bosch. The Dominican people gave Fernández his first chance to lead in 1996. His victory ended Balaguer's near monopoly on the presidency.

Fernández's first term as president was a time of economic growth for the country, but this growth ceased during the presidency of Hipólito Mejía. In 2004 the Dominican people gave Fernández a second chance as president, hoping that he could tame inflation and restore investor confidence in the country.

The National Palace, built by Trujillo in 1939, still houses government offices.

LEGISLATIVE POWER

The 1966 constitution gives all legislative powers to the bicameral National Congress, which consists of the Senate and the Chamber of Deputies. Members of both houses are directly elected for four-year terms, which are staggered across presidential terms.

The Senate has 32 seats, and the Chamber of Deputies has 150 seats. Each of the country's 31 provinces elects a senator, as does the National District. Deputies are elected by proportional representation from the provinces. A province with a large population will be represented by more deputies than one with a smaller population.

The constitution gives the congress the power to control immigration, change internal administrative boundaries, declare a state of emergency, legislate on matters of public debt and matters outside executive and judicial authority, examine presidential initiatives, levy taxes, and question cabinet ministers (although it does not confirm them for office), among others.

The legislative branch had a negligible role under the strong arm of the caudillo. Even with its constitutional powers after 1966, it remained weak during the Balaguer years. Only in 1978, with democracy fully restored under presidents Guzmán Fernández and Jorge Blanco, was the National Congress finally able to start acting on its constitutional powers. Though not yet fully independent of the president's control, it is developing as an important balance to the nation's strong executive office.

BUREAUCRACY PAYS

The Dominican Republic has no permanent civil service, so all bureaucratic positions are filled through patronage. Presidents may try to consolidate their constituencies and combat unemployment by giving government jobs to a lot of people, which leads to a rather bloated bureaucracy. Government jobs are considered very lucrative; the desirability of a particular job often depends on the potential income from bribery.

International lending agencies have pressured the government to limit public spending. Though presidents are reluctant to risk dismissing public employees, they may reduce their salaries, which invariably leads to increased corruption. Government workers in the Dominican Republic have always supplemented their salaries through bribery, but the level of corruption has risen even more with the austerity measures and salary freezes of the last two decades.

JUDICIAL POWER

The judicial branch of government is headed by a supreme court which consists of 16 members. It is the ultimate court of appeal and tries any case involving the president, vice-president, designated cabinet members, and members of congress. The supreme court also administers the entire judicial system which includes courts of first instance and courts of appeal, and can dismiss or transfer lower-court judges.

Judges serve four-year renewable terms coinciding with the presidential term. Supreme-court justices are

The Dominican judicial system is based on the Napoleonic code. Cases are tried according to reasoning based on what the code says, rather than reasoning based on historical precedent.

appointed by the National Judicial Council, consisting of the president of the Dominican Republic, leaders of both houses of the congress, the president of the supreme court, and an opposition-party member. The council was created after the 1994 elections, to curb the power of the president to appoint the highest judges in the land without consultation. The judiciary remains the weakest branch of government.

A mural campaigns for people to vote for Bosch. Although Bosch was not allowed to complete his term as president in 1963 and was never reelected, he continued to influence Dominican politics until his death in 2001.

POLITICAL PARTIES

Two main parties have dominated Dominican politics since the 1960s: the Reformist Party (PR) and the Dominican Revolutionary Party (PRD). The PRD was established in 1939 by Dominican exiles opposed to the Trujillo dictatorship. Bosch began his career in politics in the left-of-center, democratically oriented PRD, but later split and formed a more radical party, the Dominican Liberation Party (PLD). Guzmán Fernández and Blanco were elected to the presidency as members of the PRD, and Leonel Fernández was twice elected on the PLD ticket.

The other major party, the PR, served as Balaguer's personal political machine for more than two decades. Although more ideologically conservative, the party has generally served to promote patronage more than to push a particular platform.

In 1985 Balaguer promoted a union with the Revolutionary Social Christian Party (PRSC) and formed the Social Christian Reformist Party (still designated by the initials PRSC). This union gave Balaguer and his successor, Mejia, a more legitimate support base through trade unions, student groups, and campesino (rural people) organizations affiliated with the party.

In addition to the PLD, the two main political parties of the far left are the Dominican Communist Party (PCD) and the Socialist Bloc (SB).

THE ARMED FORCES

The Dominican government recognizes the importance to democracy of a professional, nonpolitical military, but the armed forces continue to influence domestic politics, although more indirectly than before. The government has, since 1978, actively worked to reduce the political role of the armed forces. Members of the armed forces and the police are not allowed to vote or to participate in the activities of political parties or labor unions.

The armed forces consist of the army, the navy, and the air force. The combined strength of these forces totals 44,000, equaling five military personnel for every 1,000 citizens. The military is involved in stopping drug trafficking and patrolling the Haitian border for illegal immigrants.

Although the Dominican Republic has not confronted any serious external threats for years, it still perceives Haiti and Cuba as potential threats to national security. Haiti is a concern due to internal political upheavals that could spill over the border in the form of refugees. The Dominican Republic does not fear an overt attack by Cuba but that Cuba will sponsor Dominican dissidents to revolt, as happened in 1959 during the Trujillo dictatorship.

The armed forces' unofficial mission is to maintain internal security and public order. Only a few underground insurgency groups remain in operation in the Dominican Republic, however, and they represent little threat to internal security.

While the national police are officially responsible for maintaining internal security, they are often aided by the armed forces. The armed forces have been summoned in the recent past to assist the police in quelling civil unrest in the form of strikes and protest rioting, especially during the 1980s and again in 2003 and 2004.

The constitution requires the armed forces to pursue civic action programs in addition to defense duties, and to participate in social and economic development projects, such as digging wells, constructing roads, building houses and schools, providing medical assistance to citizens, and protecting and replanting forests.

ECONOMY

THE ECONOMY OF THE DOMINICAN REPUBLIC is undergoing a dramatic transformation from primarily agricultural to service-oriented. These changes began in the 1980s, but the pace of change has really picked up in the last decade of the 20th century.

The main growth sectors are tourism and light manufacturing, both concentrated in coastal and urban areas. The Dominican Republic has registered some of the highest growth rates in the region, and some Dominicans have made fortunes. The downside has been increased economic volatility, and vulnerability for the poor. A decrease in the regulation of trade and banking has led to the collapse of private banks due to mismanagement. Accusations of corruption abound in politics and among the elite, while the poor have adjusted as best as they can to the rapid change and instability.

Left: **Manufacturing has been one of the sectors with the highest growth in the last 20 years.**

Opposite: **Dominicans trade at a weekly market in Elias Pinas, a town on the southwestern border.**

AGRICULTURE

Previously, agriculture was the economic foundation and the main employer in the Dominican Republic; today it accounts for only 10.7 percent of the country's gross domestic product (GDP) and employs only 17 percent of its workforce.

Historically, tight import restrictions forced the Dominicans to grow most of their own food and rely on sugar exports for the bulk of their foreign earnings. Today Dominicans import food and export many cash crops such as coffee, cocoa, and tobacco. This shift was made to increase foreign currency earnings in order to meet the requirements of international financial institutions.

Latifundios (lah-tee-FOON-dyos), or large landholdings, account for only 2 percent of Dominican farms, but they control 55 percent of the farmland. In contrast, *minifundios* (mee-nee-FOON-dyos), which are landholdings smaller than 50 acres (20 hectares), account for 82 percent of Dominican farms but occupy only 12 percent of the farmland. Tens of thousands of campesinos own no more than a few *tareas* (tah-RAY-as), a unit equivalent to 0.15 acres (0.06 hectares).

SUGAR The Dominican Republic is the 10th-largest sugar producer in the world. Sugar is its largest agricultural export. The world price of sugar and the success of the harvest have a dramatic impact on Dominicans. Tens of thousands of Dominicans in the fields, mills, refineries, distilleries, and shipyards depend on sugar for a living. Sugar prices have generally declined since 1980. Higher oil prices, global economic recessions, and greater competition among producers have pushed sugar prices down. Beet sugar produced in temperate areas, such as the United States and Europe, has reduced demand for tropical cane sugar. Hurricane Georges in 1998 devastated the main sugar-producing region around La Romana and Boca Chica.

Workers harvest sugar-cane in Puerto Plata. Like coffee and cocoa plantations, sugar plantations hire seasonal labor.

Many of the large sugar plantations are owned by private investors. There are also independent cane growers called *colonos* (koh-LOH-nohs), who sell directly to the mills. As their small landholdings become fragmented, fewer growers can survive from sugar.

COFFEE Most coffee farms in the Dominican Republic are small landholdings run by farmers who make their living growing coffee. Coffee production fell drastically following Hurricane Georges. In addition to rebuilding their farms and livelihood, small-scale coffee growers have been working to improve their farming methods with the government's assistance. Governmental initiatives were implemented to improve the quality of Dominican coffee and promote its reputation and competitiveness in world markets.

TOBACCO   First cultivated by the Taino Arawak, tobacco enjoyed a renaissance in the Dominican Republic during the 1960s with the introduction of new varieties and an increased market price. It peaked as an export crop in 1978, then declined in the 1980s due to disease, deteriorating prices, and inadequate marketing. Black tobacco is the variety that is manufactured into cigars for export. It accounts for 88 percent of the harvest.

The Dominican Republic is the world's largest cigar exporter, with exports worth about $200 million a year. More and more foreign cigar companies operate out of the Dominican Republic, taking advantage of its free-trade zones (FTZs). The earnings of these companies do not contribute directly to national accounts, but the local revenue and the jobs they offer contribute to the country's economic overall growth.

Two tobacco workers take a break from tying harvested tobacco leaves in bundles for processing.

NONTRADITIONAL CROPS Falling prices for traditional crops in the 1980s persuaded the Dominican government to promote nontraditional crop exports. Successful nontraditional crops include ornamental plants, winter vegetables (vegetables not grown in the United States in winter), citrus and tropical fruit, spices, nuts, and the distinctive produce popular with the Hispanic population in the United States. The conversion to nontraditional crops was aided by the Caribbean Basin Initiative, which provided duty-free access to the U.S. market for some 3,000 products.

FOOD CROPS Rice, the main ingredient in the national dish, was the Dominican Republic's most important food crop. Rice production in the country has fallen since 1979 and can no longer meet domestic demand, forcing the country to import.

Other major food crops include corn (which is native to the island), sorghum, plantains, beans, and assorted tubers. Dominican farmers also grow various kinds of fruit, vegetables, spices, and nuts, including bananas, guavas, tamarinds, passionfruit, coconuts, tomatoes, carrots, lettuce, cabbages, scallions, onions, garlic, coriander, and peanuts.

LIVESTOCK The Dominican Republic raises enough livestock for domestic use as well as export. Livestock ranches consist primarily of beef and dairy cattle, poultry, and swine. Cattle ranching, the basis of the economy in the mid-19th century, remains important. The main export commodities are hides and salted beef.

Picking beans on a collective farm in southern Dominican Republic.

FORESTRY

The government prohibited commercial tree cutting in 1967 to counter the effects of slash-and-burn agriculture and indiscriminate tree cutting. The remaining forests, covering only 22 percent of the land, consist mainly of pine and hardwood.

Plantation forestry provides timber products for domestic use, but wood products are still imported to meet demand. The government is working toward replacing some of the lost forest.

Salt is produced for the domestic market by letting the sun evaporate saltwater.

MINING

The Dominican Republic's most important minerals include ferronickel, bauxite, and a gold-silver alloy called Dore. Lesser minerals include iron, limestone, copper, gypsum, mercury, salt, sulfur, marble, onyx, and travertine. Marble, onyx, and travertine are industrial minerals.

The government fueled a rapid growth in the mining sector during the 1970s when it invited foreign companies to search for minerals. The second largest ferronickel mine in the world is the Falcondo Mine in Bonao, northwest of Santo Domingo, and ferronickel is the country's biggest mineral export.

MANUFACTURING

Manufacturing accounts for nearly a third of the GDP and employs a quarter of the workforce. Food and beverage processing make up more than half of Dominican manufacturing activities. Manufacturing firms also produce chemicals, textiles, and nonmetallic minerals.

Along with many developing countries, the Dominican Republic has opened its doors to FTZs, areas that are given special status so that

businesses producing goods within them are not subject to taxes. It is as if the FTZ is not part of the country in which it is located. FTZs in the Dominican Republic tend to be built near ports. Foreign businesses import parts, assemble products in the FTZs, and export the products to their destination markets.

FTZ expansion in the Dominican Republic has been phenomenal, bringing foreign investment and innovation, but jobs in FTZs usually pay poorly. While many Dominican women benefit from holding non-traditional jobs in FTZs, tension may develop in some homes where the woman earns more than her underemployed husband. The frequency of marriage breakdowns increased, as has the proportion of households headed by women, now 29 percent of all households.

The main FTZ industries in the Dominican Republic are clothing, electronics, footwear, jewelry, furniture, perfume, and pharmaceuticals. FTZs also contain call centers and data-entry enterprises, which have bolstered jobs in the service sector. One of the newest FTZs being developed is the Cyber Park near Santo Domingo. It will house computer firms, a golf course, and a training school for workers.

CONSTRUCTION

The construction sector enjoyed rapid growth in the 1970s and 1980s. By 1991, however, it accounted for only 7.1 percent of the GDP and 4.5 percent of the workforce. Construction picked up in the late 1990s to become one of the country's main areas of growth by 2002, with a growth rate of 3.2 percent.

The government generated considerable construction activity in the 1980s through such projects as renovating the old section of Santo Domingo, building the Columbus Lighthouse, and developing a new suburb. The construction industry is generally self-sufficient, since its most important materials are produced domestically.

ENERGY

With no oil or coal of its own, the Dominican Republic struggles with an energy problem. Some of its rivers produce hydroelectric power but not enough for the demands of a growing population and economy. High energy prices and rolling blackouts are common.

TOURISM

Every year, 3 million tourists, mostly from the United States, Canada, and Europe, visit the

Dominican Republic, using goods and services worth $1.5 billion. With relaxed investment regulations, many new resorts have sprung up. While tourism creates jobs, it strains the infrastructure and is unpredictable and vulnerable to global economic ups and downs. On the bright side, tourism is a good incentive for the country to protect its natural environment.

BOOM AND BUST

The Dominican Republic has experienced some of the most dramatic growth rates in the Caribbean as a result of expanded tourism and FTZ investment. Those well-placed to take advantage of these booms have become wealthy, but neither sector has produced stable, permanent, well-paid jobs in significant numbers, so most Dominicans have not benefited much. The country is still plagued by serious inequalities, with the richest 10 percent earning 38 percent of the wealth and the poorest 10 percent earning 2.1 percent. Rapid growth also fostered irregularities in investment and accounting, which caused bank failures in 2003. The nation has to find a balance between economic growth and stability so that poor Dominicans can get a chance at a better life.

Above: **The government began promoting tourism in 1971 with the Tourist Incentive Law. The effort has paid off in many respects, but shortages of clean water, electricity, and building materials continue to interfere with the industry's success.**

Opposite: **The republic boasts many seaports capable of handling international and domestic trade, making shipping the island's main mode of commercial transportation.**

ENVIRONMENT

THE DOMINICAN REPUBLIC, like all island nations, faces difficult environmental challenges because both land and fresh water are limited. Rapid population growth and urbanization create acute problems when fresh water is scarce and when there are no vast stretches of unoccupied land to absorb waste. The situation becomes even more complicated when the economy depends on clean oceans and beaches to attract tourists.

In the 21st century, key environmental issues for the people of this beautiful island revolve around pollution control, waste management, the use of precious fresh water, and the preservation of critical fragile ecosystems. Fortunately, Dominicans are beginning to take steps to reverse environmental damage and adopt more sustainable practices.

Left: **Strong winds shake the trees and whip the waters at Santo Domingo in the wake of Hurricane Bonnie on August 25, 1998.**

Opposite: **The Chavón River in the Dominican Republic.**

Wooden fishing boats at Boca Chica, one of many beautiful beaches in the Dominican Republic.

WATER, WATER EVERYWHERE

The Dominican Republic is surrounded by water, but water is a scarce resource on the island. Saltwater sustains only certain forms of life; land plants and animals, including humans, require fresh water to survive.

Dominicans get the fresh water they need from rain. Most rain falls on the highlands, where rivers carry the water into the lowlands and out to sea. Most rain is caused by ocean and air currents, but research suggests that tropical forests can contribute to the conditions necessary for rainfall through the release of water from the leaves of trees and by creating updrafts of cooler air. Also, the roots of trees anchor the soil so that it acts like a sponge, absorbing rainwater that would otherwise wash the soil away.

Human activity easily upsets this delicate natural system. Forests are cleared to make way for farms to grow crops to feed the growing population, and, without alternative sources of energy, wood is used as fuel for cooking. If there are no tree roots to absorb rainwater, raging rivers form that can cause floods and destroy human settlements; soil is washed out to sea, where it can choke coral reefs and kill fish.

Dominican waterways need protection from pollution. Pesticides used on plantations get washed by rain into rivers, which become more contaminated when urban sewage is dumped into them. This flows out to sea, where it destroys marine life and makes swimming hazardous.

Without vibrant coral reefs and clean beaches to draw tourists to the coastal resorts, urban dwellers have fewer jobs. If safeguards are not implemented to protect waterways, Dominicans risk destroying the ecosystems that sustain life. Their challenge in the immediate future is to balance competing uses of fresh water with everyone's dependence on it to make their living.

A bridge carries traffic across the Ozama River in Santo Domingo. Waterways offer beautiful scenery to residents and commuters, but human activity often pollutes them.

FIRST STEPS IN ENVIRONMENTAL PROTECTION

From the time of Columbus to the 1960s, about 77 percent of the Dominican Republic's original forest cover was cleared to make way for plantations and then the lumber industry. In the 1960s the government banned commercial logging and started forest reserves and parks. This dramatically slowed, but did not stop, deforestation. People in rural areas still needed wood for fuel and land to farm.

In 2000, for the first time in decades, the government addressed environmental policy and passed the Environmental Framework Law. The law created the first Dominican Ministry of the Environment and Natural Resources, which is charged with regulating the use of natural resources such as water and forests. Its mandate is to seek cooperation from private business interests and communities in creating sustainable practices that balance competing human needs with the requirements

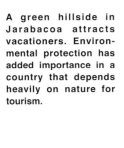

A green hillside in Jarabacoa attracts vacationers. Environmental protection has added importance in a country that depends heavily on nature for tourism.

of preservation. There are signs that Dominicans will find a way to live within the limits set by nature. For example, the Sabana Yegua Model Forest, set up in 2003, offers a novel approach to forest management. Rather than stay out of the forest altogether, the local people learn to cut trees selectively and to plant consistently so that there is always a supply of trees for wood and fuel.

People are also encouraged to plant fruit and nut trees so that they benefit from the living forest rather than earning a living by the death of the forest. Learning how to use the forest instead of seeing it as an obstruction to farming and other activities encourages people to get involved in forest maintenance. Protecting the forest guarantees less soil erosion and more fresh water for all Dominicans. It has the added advantage of reducing the risk of flooding and damage to coral reefs. Such an integrated approach benefits everyone.

Agricultural workers in Azua load crates full of tomatoes onto trucks. Farmers seek to maintain a balance that enables Dominicans to enjoy the fruits of nature without destroying it.

FUTURE OF ENVIRONMENTAL PROTECTION

The Dominican Republic is a small country with big environmental challenges. The government is implementing projects that meet the needs of all parties and encourage conservation as part of long-term economic management.

In the end, Dominicans will benefit from cleaner water, healthier forests, and the money visitors spend to enjoy this island paradise. The Dominican Republic receives 3 million tourists every year and earns about $1.5 billion from tourism. One of the fastest-growing sectors of the economy, tourism provides a strong incentive for environmental protection, because so much is at stake.

Tourists enjoy a river-fed pool in the Dominican Republic.

One of the Dominican Republic's protected natural attractions are the whales in the Bay of Samaná. Every year from January to March 10,000 North Atlantic humpback whales come to the warmer waters of the Caribbean to perform their intricate mating dance and give birth to the next generation. Whales must surface every 15 to 45 minutes to breathe. Humpbacks, being fairly slow-moving, especially in shallow waters, have been easy targets for whalers. In 1966 they became protected by the International Whaling Commission. Today it is estimated that there are about 35,000 to 40,000 humpbacks worldwide, or about 35 percent of their peak population.

THE HUMPBACKS OF SAMANÁ

Humpbacks are a delight to watch because they are very active and visible. They sometimes breach, or throw their entire body out of the water, and they can swim upside down with their fins out of the water. Also, they communicate by raising their huge tails out of the water and slapping them down. Many people have heard their famous "songs," patterned sequences of noises that males sometimes emit while hanging their head down in deep water. Scientists do not know what the songs are for, but all whales in the same population, such as those in the North Atlantic, sing the same song, which is distinct from the songs sung by other populations, such as those in the North Pacific. Humpbacks spend part of the year in the frigid waters of the Arctic, where they feed on small organisms that they strain through the baleen in their mouths. They migrate to warmer and shallower waters, such as those around Hispaniola and in the Bay of Samaná, so that fertile females can mate and give birth. During this period, whales fast, since there is no food in the water for them. A humpback calf weighs about a ton at birth and will stay with its mother for the first year of life. She will protect it and nurse it with her rich milk. While mother and calf are in warm water, the mother does not eat, while the calf can consume up to 100 gallons of her milk a day. All adult whales lose about 25 percent of their body weight during their tropical water visits, while calves gain up to 100 pounds every day in preparation for their first trip into colder waters.

DOMINICANS

TWO CHARACTERISTICS that readily define Dominican society are extremes of wealth and poverty, and the consciousness of skin color. Light-skinned Dominicans identify themselves as white, and those of mixed ancestry call themselves Indian. Although race divides Dominican society to a lesser degree than does economic status, upper-class Dominicans tend to have lighter skin that Dominicans in the lower classes. This is a reflection of the historical correspondence of race and class.

Opposite: **A trio of little Dominican girls.**

Below: **Two Dominican boys have a little fun mimicking a grotesque painting on a pillar.**

Above and opposite: **The tendency to ignore their African cultural roots developed among the people of the Dominican Republic primarily in the 20th century.**

RACE AND CLASS

Although the Dominican Republic was Spain's oldest colony in the Americas, it has the shallowest genealogical roots. Spaniards came to the island seeking gold or land, but they often moved on to mainland America for economic or political reasons. Thus, for many white Dominicans, their ancestry on Hispaniola spans no more than six generations. Historically, the black population was anchored by slavery and servitude, but these same institutions made it difficult to trace the lineage of black Dominicans. More recently, Dominicans of all colors and classes have migrated from the island's rural areas to its cities and beyond, such as Puerto Rico and mainland America.

Only 16 percent of the Dominican population is white or of pure European ancestry. The proportion of blacks is even lower—only 11 percent. About 73 percent of the population is of mixed ancestry. Immigrants make up a tiny proportion of the island's population, but they come from near and far: Haiti, the West Indies, the United States, Lebanon, Italy, France, China, and Japan.

Although more than two-thirds of Dominican society is mulatto, of mixed black and white ancestry, most Dominicans deny their African ancestry and ignore African influences on their culture. In the 1880s, some intellectuals advocated a celebration of mulatto culture, but such racial pride was swept away during Trujillo's rule.

A mulatto himself, Trujillo rewrote Dominican history and racial identities to deny African elements in the population and culture. He created a national ideology of *hispanidad* (ees-pah-nee-DAHD), which defined Dominicans as the most Spanish people of America.

Today Dominicans identify themselves as either white or Indian. Official identification cards do not mention mulattos, and the term black is reserved for Haitians. Dominicans like to describe their skin color as *café con leche*, or coffee with milk, but they attribute this to their Indian background.

The military is one of few avenues for upward social and economic mobility for poor Dominicans. In fact, the Dominican Republic has had more black and mulatto presidents than any other Western Hispanic nation.

A small, elite group commands a great proportion of Dominican wealth and power, while the majority of the population lives in poverty. Socially, the primary division is between the gentility—called *la gente buena* (la HEN-tay BUAY-nah), literally good people, or *la gente culta* (la HEN-tay KOOL-tah), literally refined people—and the common masses. While the masses struggle from day to day, *la gente buena* adhere to traditional Hispanic ideals of dignity, leisure, grandeur, and generosity.

UPPER CLASS

The Dominican Republic did not develop a true landowning class until the late 1800s, almost 200 years later than most Latin American countries. The primary source of social identity for the mostly white oligarchy is through kinship ties, which also provide the pool from which business partners and political allies are selected.

In Santo Domingo and Santiago, the upper class is divided into two sections: *la gente de primera* (la HEN-tay day pree-MAY-rah), or first people; and *la gente de segunda* (la HEN-tay day say-GOON-dah), or second people. *La gente de primera* include 100 families that constitute the cream of the upper class. They are locally referred to as the *tutumpote* (too-toom-POH-tay), or totem pole, implying family worship and excessive concern with ancestry. *La gente de segunda* include descendants of the business elite that emerged in the early 20th century, and the *nuevos ricos* (NUAY-vohs REE-kohs), or new rich, who emerged with the rise of Trujillo. The newest elites have acquired their wealth through banking, professional occupations, light industry, and tourism.

The upper class concerns itself with national and international issues, such as world sugar prices, U.S. power and investments, trade patterns, the future of tourism, the need for social and political order and improved infrastructure, and the complex web of family ties and associated gossip.

The composition of the Dominican oligarchy continually shifted with each new political or economic wave as members of the upper class emigrated.

MIDDLE CLASS

The expansion of the sugar industry in the late 19th century broadened the ranks of the middle class to include professionals, small shopkeepers, teachers, and clerical employees. Today, the middle class constitutes 30 to 35 percent of the population and is concentrated among the salaried professionals in the government and private sectors.

The middle class lacks a sense of class identity partly due to the fact that its members rely on the patron-client system to move ahead rather than on any common bond of social or economic interest. Moreover, those with dark skin or limited finances have limited opportunities for social mobility. The upper-middle class is mostly white, but most middle-class Dominicans are mulattos.

The members of the middle class like to consider themselves part of *la gente buena*, at least in spirit. To the extent that they are able, they adopt the attitudes and lifestyle espoused by the elites. However, they have no independent sources of wealth and are vulnerable to the economic cycles of the country. This reinforces the patron-client system, since they must rely on patronage rather than political action when ill winds blow.

The concerns of the middle class center on expanding their wealth and extending their network of social and political influence. As they rise, they are in turn expected to reward their family and friends.

Small shopkeepers and salaried professionals make up most of the middle class.

61

Most Dominican mulattos and blacks count themselves among the rural and urban working class.

LOWER CLASS

The concerns of two-thirds of Dominicans center on issues of daily survival. Mostly illiterate and unskilled, they struggle for food, shelter, and clothing, because there are not enough jobs to go around. A quarter of them are unemployed.

RURAL POOR Two types of campesinos characterize the countryside: subsistence farmers and landless wage workers. For every small landholder, there are 10 to 20 wage workers competing for whatever jobs are available. Most small rural neighborhoods in the country are very close-knit. They were originally settled by one or two families whose descendants developed extensive kinship ties through intermarriage and *compadrazgo* (kom-pah-DRAHZ-goh), or godparentage. Campesinos usually live close to a water source in small groups of houses connected by narrow dirt paths. They depend on their neighbors and kin for assistance and tend to distrust outsiders.

Among the Dominican rural poor, almost all women contribute to the family income, and they are increasingly left to run the household alone as the men leave to seek work. The women earn money by cultivating garden plots, raising livestock for sale, and selling various items from lottery tickets to homemade sweets. They also work during the labor-intensive phases of harvesting cotton, coffee, and tobacco, but they earn less than their male counterparts and are paid by the unit rather than on a daily basis.

URBAN POOR In 1920, 80 percent of Dominicans lived in rural areas. Today, 67 percent live in rapidly expanding cities. Most of this migration happened after 1970.

Campunos (kahm-POO-nohs), or rural-to-urban migrants, are seeking employment, but they find instead overcrowded slums with malnourished children, no electricity, no running water, and no sewage facilities. National unemployment runs at 16.5 percent, and 25 percent of the population lives in poverty. The rate of underemployment is even higher; many have jobs but cannot earn enough for their needs. A large proportion of urban households are headed by women who often earn money more consistently than men.

Small neighborhoods are the center of social life for the urban poor. As in the rest of Dominican society, the urban poor turn to neighbors and kin for assistance in times of need. Migrants maintain ties with their family back in the countryside through a *cadena* (kah-DAY-nah), or chain, of mutual assistance. People in the countryside take care of the family or land of those who leave, while people in the city help new *campunos* find work and a place to stay.

Women earn money by taking in washing, ironing, sewing, or other housework. They might also buy cheap or used items and raffle them off for a small profit, or run a sidewalk stall selling cooked food, groceries, or cigarettes and candy.

HAITIANS

There are about 500,000 Haitians and Dominicans of Haitian descent living in the Dominican Republic. Most came as agricultural workers to cut sugarcane or harvest coffee, rice, or tomatoes. Some came to escape the grinding poverty of Haiti, while others were recruited by Dominican agents known as *buscones* (boos-KOHN-ays). Haiti has been a source of cheap labor for the Dominican Republic for decades, until, in 1986, a formal agreement between the two countries permitted a fixed number of Haitians to cross the border to work.

With the privatization of government industries, the already miserable conditions of Haitian cane cutters got worse. They live in *bateyes* (bah-TAY-ays), settlements around the fields in Barahona, Puerto Plata, and Santo Domingo, in tiny shacks with no sanitation. They work 13 hours a day for very little pay, and children sometimes work alongside adults.

They have no security; the government may repatriate them anytime to appease racism and xenophobia among Dominicans. With the economic downturn in the 21st century, Haitians, Dominicans of Haitian descent, and blacks in general have been blamed for lowering wages and taking jobs. They are regularly rounded up in the thousands by the military and trucked across the border. International human-rights organizations are involved in defending these people's legal rights.

EMIGRANTS

The 2000 U.S. population census showed 692,000 people of Dominican origin living in the United States. They represent about 8 percent of the population of the Dominican Republic today. Most Dominicans in the United States live in urban centers, especially New York.

Many Dominicans start their journey by illegally emigrating to Puerto Rico in open boats known as *yolas* (YOH-lahs) across the dangerous currents of the 90-mile (145-km) Mona Passage. They pay boat runners as much as $500 for a place in a cheaply made wooden boat roughly 30 feet (9.1 m) in length and capable of holding more than 50 people.

Most Dominicans migrate to the United States to earn more money, continue their education, or join family who have already made the transition. Most of the Dominican Republic's emigrants are from urban areas. They are better-educated and more skilled than the majority of the Dominican populace.

Dominicans in the United States maintain strong ties with family back in their homeland. They feel a strong sense of obligation and regularly send money to their families. Remittances from the United States form a substantial part of the Dominican economy, contributing about $1.5 billion—the same as the tourism industry.

Angered by discrimination against African Americans in the 1960s and 1970s, many emigrants to the United States returned to the Dominican Republic wearing Afro hairstyles and other symbols of the Black Pride movement.

LIFESTYLE

DOMINICANS MANAGE to maintain an attitude of cheerful resignation in the face of extreme hardship. They may struggle for food, housing, and employment, but their quality of life often depends on how much they can share their burdens and resources with family and friends.

In the Dominican Republic, wealth reinforces power, but true power comes from a network of influential personal relationships. Dominicans of all classes greatly depend on kinship ties for land, employment, child care, economic assistance, and political positions.

Although men hold most of the political and economic power in the Dominican Republic, many identify the country as a matriarchal society typical of the Caribbean. The women are strong and bear a great deal of responsibility in everyday life.

Left: **Increasing numbers of Dominican women raise their families alone, but they are rarely rewarded for their strength and responsibility. They are paid less than men, though they often find work more regularly.**

Opposite: **A Dominican boy enjoys a cool splash under a standpipe.**

BIRTH

A particular set of customs and beliefs, affecting both mother and child, accompany the birth process, especially in rural areas and among the lower classes. For example, in many areas, the mother must avoid eating fruit (especially bananas) when pregnant lest the baby be born with phlegm in the chest. She must also abstain from eating charred or crusty food that gets stuck to the cooking kettle, in order to prevent the placenta from adhering to the uterus. It is believed that the placenta will adhere to the womb also if anyone walks behind the mother after the seventh month of pregnancy. If both husband and wife are dark in color, the pregnant woman is encouraged to drink the fistula of the Cassia plant dissolved in boiled milk; this is believed to purify the fetus so that the child will be born "almost white."

As soon as the first labor pains are felt, the woman or the midwife takes an image of Saint Raymond and places it upside down with a candle burning in front of it. As soon as the baby is born, the saint is restored to the upright position, but the candle may remain burning for a while. The mother strictly observes 40 days of confinement after the birth, during which time fresh air is excluded from her room as much as possible, and her ears are plugged with cotton. No one who has been exposed to the night air or the moonlight may enter her room for fear of causing her to suffer from *pasmo* (PAHS-moh), a term loosely applied to many illnesses, including tetanus and puerperal fever.

The mother does not nurse the baby for the first three days. She feeds the baby with a decoction made from dried rose petals with a drop of almond oil. Nor does she clip the baby's fingernails until the baby is baptized, or, it is believed, the baby will grow into a thief. The umbilical cord is kept until the child is 7 years old; it is then given to the child, who must cut it lengthwise with a knife, to open the ways of life.

HEALTH CARE

The majority of Dominicans live in unsanitary conditions with inadequate health services and poor nutrition. Health care tends to lack national coordination and management. Consequently, infectious and parasitic diseases are common.

Many Dominicans in rural areas rely on home remedies and traditional healers for their medical care. Medical services, such as hospitals, are not as available as in cities such as Santo Domingo and Santiago. Even if they were, not many can afford to patronize them.

Life expectancy has improved in the last quarter century from an average of 62.6 years in 1980 to 67.6 years in 2004. On average, life expectancy is 66 years for men and 69 years for women.

Infant mortality rates rose and fell in the same period, reaching 56 deaths per 1,000 live births in 1992 and declining to 33 in 2004, still higher than the 1982 rate of 31.7.

GROWING UP

Dominican children often draw their playmates and friends from a large pool of cousins and siblings. Since members of the extended family often live close to one another, cousins play together as closely as brothers and sisters. In Dominican society, parents consider it very important to give birth to at least one son, and many discipline their sons less strictly than their daughters. Girls are closely chaperoned by the whole family, and their brothers and male cousins are expected to protect them and their reputations.

Many children, both in the countryside and in the cities, must work to supplement the family's income. Poor children bear heavy responsibility and have little time for fun and games. Campesino girls help their mothers cook and clean, while boys work beside their fathers in the fields.

In the cities, boys work long hours selling newspapers or shining shoes, while girls sell flowers, gum, and other small candies. Children, even as young as 7 or 8 years old, often work alone.

Children of wealthy families are closely supervised. After school, they may engage in formal lessons, such as art or piano, or play organized sports or informal games. Boys start playing baseball almost as soon as they can walk, and they join local baseball teams when they are 6 or 7 years old. Wealthy parents may send their older children to private college preparatory or high schools in the United States.

In wealthier families, girls often celebrate their 15th birthday, or *quinciñera* (keen-see-NYAY-rah), with a large party. Although not as formal in the Dominican Republic as in some Latin American countries, the custom still signifies the girl's transition to adulthood. Less common

in recent years, the *quinciñera* is increasingly being replaced by a social celebration at age 16, when the girl makes her debut as a woman in Dominican society.

Young Dominicans love going out at night in large groups. In the big cities, they go to the movies and dance clubs, eat ice cream, or just spend time together gossiping, flirting, driving up and down the main avenue, and generally having a good time. More conservative parents do not allow their children, especially their daughters, to go on dates without a chaperon. Many couples, or *novios* (NOH-byohs), date in groups, with friends who can act as chaperons. Young women pay a lot of attention to their appearance, venturing out in dresses and high heels, and with carefully coifed hair and decorative jewelry. Young men dress in style as well and liberally spray themselves with cologne. They guard the behavior of their girlfriends and sisters jealously, but they flirt animatedly with other girls.

Schoolchildren playing in the eastern Dominican Republic.

Dominican males strive to look macho.

GENDER ROLES

Gender roles in the Dominican Republic tend to be defined by the concept of machismo, or masculine pride. Men are often concerned with conforming to a macho image. They strive to appear strong and domineering, but are rather conscious of how they appear when others are looking. They may try to reinforce their macho image and self-image by maintaining a strong camaraderie with other men and by making sexual comments to passing females.

Machismo is also characterized by sexual prowess, so that many Dominican men carry on romantic affairs outside their marriages. Moreover, there is no shame for a man to have children out of wedlock as long as he takes responsibility for them. Machismo also dictates that a man should be the head of the family and support his children, whether legitimate or not.

Women, on the other hand, are expected to be docile, protected, virtuous, and submissive. Nonetheless, more and more women are working outside the home, and a large number of families are headed by women, as many fathers are not around or have limited economic assets. An increasing number of women have also started entering politics. Former president Balaguer was instrumental in this, because he appointed women governors in every province.

Traditional gender roles are introduced at an early age and reinforced on a daily basis as children grow up. Among the poor, little boys are often allowed to run around naked and play unsupervised in large groups of friends. When they grow up, they are expected to have premarital and extramarital affairs, but girls are carefully groomed and closely chaperoned, and they are expected to be quiet and helpful and, most of all, to stay virtuous before and during marriage.

Mothers are greatly revered in the Dominican Republic, and the mother-child relationship is generally considered pure and indestructible. Mothers are openly affectionate with their children. Fathers, on the other hand, are generally more removed from day-to-day family affairs. They are seen as authority figures to be obeyed and respected without question.

Dominican women's roles are changing.

MARRIAGE NAMES

Many Dominicans follow the Spanish custom of having a double surname, taking the patrimonial surname from both parents to form their own surname. A noted Dominican literary family provides a good example of the patrilineal distribution of family names. Dominican poet Nicolás Ureña de Mendoza had three names: Nicolás was his first name; Ureña was his father's surname, which he also passed on to his children; and de Mendoza was his mother's surname, which his children did not inherit. His daughter, poet Salomé Ureña, married journalist and politician Francisco Henríquez y Carvajal, becoming Salomé Ureña de Henríquez. Their sons, named Pedro Henríquez Ureña and Max Henríquez Ureña, became distinguished literary critics and historians.

MARRIAGE AND FAMILY

Rural families tend to be more stable, and the women more independent. Because marriage unites not only the bride and groom, but also their families, the husband's work is often tied to his wife's family. If he leaves his wife, he loses his source of income as well.

The ideal Dominican marriage process involves a man asking a virtuous young woman to marry him. They have a formal engagement followed by a religious wedding in a lavishly decorated church, which concludes with an elaborate fiesta, attended by throngs of relatives and friends. In modern Dominican society, this ideal, if realized at all, is generally reserved for the middle and upper classes. The frequency of free unions, or common-law marriages, demonstrates that the ideal marriage process usually involves resources that poor Dominicans cannot afford.

There are three types of long-term union in the Dominican Republic: civil, religious, and common-law marriages. Close to 80 percent of young Dominicans join in free unions, and approximately half of them break up while still in their 20s. Upon dissolution of a free union, the only property that the woman receives is the house, if the couple owned one. She may receive child support only if the father legally recognizes the children. Most poor Dominicans cannot afford to marry officially, especially when they are young. Many of them later marry someone in a civil or religious ceremony, however, if they have a bit more economic security.

Civil marriages performed by the state are the most common. This is probably because annulments are very difficult and expensive to obtain through the Roman Catholic Church, while divorce is relatively easy to obtain from the government.

Kinship ties, extended through the system of godparents, constitute a major source of political and economic power in Dominican society. Parents choose the godparents, or *compadres* (kom-PAH-drays), a few months before the birth of their child. The selection depends not only on the character and friendship of the godparents-to-be but on their financial situation as well. The *compadres* are not only to guide the child spiritually but also to help him or her economically. They are expected to assist in paying for the baptism ceremony and celebration, and often assume financial responsibility for the child's education, medical care, marriage, and even funeral. Throughout his or her life, a godchild has the right to ask his or her *compadres* for financial aid.

The godparents treat their godchild with great affection, often to the extent of tolerating mischief and hiding misbehavior from the parents, especially if the child is a boy. In turn, the child treats the godparents with a mixture of respect and affection.

The parents and the godparents also share a special relationship, treating each other with extreme reverence and formality, even if they were very close friends before the child's baptism.

While the Dominican family is being transformed by migration and urbanization, kinship ties remain very important. Individuals moving from the countryside or small towns to the city or to the United States depend on their family and friends to help them adapt. They in turn try to help their family at home by sending them money.

EDUCATION

Eighty-five percent of the Dominican population is literate, an increase from 74 percent of the population in 1986. The Secretariat of State for Education and Welfare administers the system of education and requires Dominican children to attend at least six years of primary school, beginning at age 7. In rural areas, however, not all schools offer all six grades to their communities. Preschool education is available in some areas but is not compulsory.

Secondary education is not compulsory either, and only about two-thirds of the population attend, beginning at age 13. Most of those who continue their education beyond secondary school train for university admission, and some attend teacher-training, polytechnic, or vocational schools. Many of the secondary educational programs suffer from low academic standards and high drop-out rates. Most students are required to buy their own textbooks, which dissuades many from enrolling. Many urban middle-class families send their children to private secondary schools, most of which are operated by the Roman Catholic Church.

There are eight universities and a total of more than 26 institutions of higher education in the Dominican Republic. Many wealthy families send their children to schools in the United States.

The Universitas Santi Dominici in the capital was established by Spanish missionaries. The Church continues to play a large role in education in the Dominican Republic. In the 1960s, the Church was involved in the government's adult literacy program.

The Dominican Republic's only public university is the Autonomous University of Santo Domingo (UASD). It traces its roots directly to the Universitas Santi Dominici, which the Spanish established in 1538 as the first university in the Americas. The UASD has for decades been the hub of student political activity and government opposition. Whereas the battles of the 1960s concerned human rights, students today focus on budget issues.

The leading private universities include the Catholic University Mother and Teacher (UCMM) and the Pedro Henríquez Ureña National University (UNPHU). The UCMM is administered by the Roman Catholic Church in Santiago. The UNPHU is a technical university in Santo Domingo. These private universities tend to enroll students who are wealthier and less occupied with political issues.

HOUSING

The Dominican Republic suffers from an urban housing crisis. Urban development cannot keep up with the level of migration to the cities, condemning thousands of poor Dominicans to makeshift shelters in open lots or abandoned buildings. Rural housing varies from upper-class estates, to the most primitive barracks for sugarcane workers.

RURAL HOUSING Many agricultural plantations hire large numbers of temporary workers for the harvest. The majority of these workers are provided with stark housing. They sleep in overcrowded concrete barracks with no water, electricity, or sewage facilities.

More permanent agricultural workers are often allowed to live on company land in small shacks called *bohíos* (boh-EE-ohs). In the more prosperous Cibao region, houses are built of solid palm board or pine.

TRANSPORTATION

Overcrowded buses and vans tear through the streets of Santo Domingo or, alternatively, crawl along in its heavy traffic. Since the fares on these conveyances are relatively low, the majority of Dominicans in the city use them to go back and forth to work and to do their shopping. On special occasions, those who can afford it might take a taxi. Only wealthy Dominicans can afford to own a car.

Santo Domingo is the hub of a transportation system that carries people and goods to almost anywhere in the country. Most goods are transported by truck to the major market centers, although a government-owned railroad also carries freight through the eastern half of the Cibao, from La Vega to the port of Sánchez on the Bay of Samaná. In the absence of a passenger railway, people travel by bus or car within the country. The other railroads, publicly and privately owned, primarily serve the sugar industry.

The most common means of transportation in the rural and suburban parts of the Dominican Republic is the motorcycle or riding in the back of a pickup truck.

The occupants paint the houses in unusually bright colors with vividly contrasting shutters and lintels. The roofs are made of simple materials such as sheets of zinc or tin, or they might be thatched in poorer households. Most rural Dominicans live on packed earthen floors, although the better off sometimes have concrete floors.

URBAN HOUSING Squatter settlements are rapidly spreading around the edges of the major cities. People move from smaller towns or from the countryside and establish a tenuous foothold in the urban areas by building a shelter out of whatever materials they can gather, such as cardboard or discarded inner tubes.

Wealthier Dominicans live in modern houses in nice neighborhoods, often protecting their properties with security gates and high walls.

DEATH

If a person becomes seriously ill, close relatives and intimate friends congregate at the patient's house. Most of them stay there day and night until after the funeral or until the person recovers. They relieve the patient's family of all duties and responsibilities by ministering to the patient's needs as well as doing the housework.

As soon as a person is pronounced dead, all receptacles that contain water must be emptied at once. Campesinos believe that the ghost bathes in every available vessel in the house, even in the drinking gourd. They consider it "bad" to use such water. The attendants also shut or block the front door of the house for nine days, or *la novena* (la noh-BAY-nah), during which time one can enter the house only through the back door, even if it means tearing down a fence to get to it.

Finally, the family covers all mirrors or turns them against the wall to prevent anyone from seeing a reflection of the ghost's image, which,

Mourners carry flowers and crosses in a funeral procession.

they believe, will drive them insane. The family of the deceased crowds into one room with the corpse and remains there until the funeral the next day. They place the corpse in a casket, the feet facing the front of the house, with two candles at each end of the casket.

Close family members sit in the house with the corpse, praying, crying, and singing. They discuss all the good qualities of the deceased, recounting even the smallest good deed. The mourners, especially the women, dress in black or grey. In rural areas, the mourning tends to be especially intense, often with experienced wailers who utter loud mournful cries and go into hysterical fits at the sight of the corpse. The wailing continues until the corpse is taken out for the funeral.

Concrete crosses mark a cemetery in the southern Dominican Republic.

Outside the house, friends and family gather in support of the mourners. The atmosphere outside is often lighter. People tell stories of the deceased, laugh, eat, tell riddles, and even play dominoes.

At the end of the ninth day of *la novena*, the mourners will hold a ceremony called *la vela de muerto* (la BAY-lah day MOOAIR-toh)—the vigil for the dead. More common among the less educated and in the smaller towns, the ceremony varies in size and style. In more elaborate versions, the mourners renew their wailing, praying, and singing, and construct a small altar surrounded by one to four candles or lanterns. On the altar, they place a crucifix or a picture of a saint, a small pair of scissors to trim the candles, a small saucer in which to put the candle trimmings, a small receptacle for money offerings, and a glass of water for the ghost. On the first death anniversary, the family and friends commemorate the deceased with a similar ceremony.

RELIGION

A SMALL PERCENTAGE OF DOMINICANS are Protestant, and even fewer—mainly Haitian immigrants and their descendants—are followers of folk religions such as voodoo. Most Dominicans profess affiliation with the Roman Catholic Church, although few attend Mass regularly.

For Dominicans, religious practice tends to be rather formal, based more on rote memorization than on spontaneous expression. Popular religious practices differ from orthodox Catholic practices, and many Dominicans mix elements of Catholicism with folk spirituality. Saints play an important role in popular spiritual devotions, and Dominicans approach their creator almost exclusively through an intermediary—a priest or a folk spiritualist.

The Dominican Republic has one archdiocese in Santo Domingo and another in Santiago. There are nine dioceses and one military ordinariate for the armed forces. With one priest to every 10,000 Catholics, the country has the fourth highest priest-to-parishioner ratio in Latin America. The church hierarchy tends to be orthodox in outlook and procedure, while many of the parish priests are more liberal, engaging in community development projects and forming Christian base communities. These are groups of people who practice religious devotions and work to improve the community socially and economically. These priests try to forge a closer bond with the people.

The Church has lost a lot of its former influence in the Dominican Republic. Understaffed and underfunded, it no longer offers the wide variety of programs it once did. While the Church supposedly still carries some political weight on social issues such as divorce and birth control, the country has extremely permissive divorce laws and public family planning centers.

Opposite: **Built in the early 16th century, Santa María la Menor is the oldest cathedral in the Americas.**

HISTORICAL DEVELOPMENT OF THE CHURCH

During the first century after colonization, Dominican friars and other missionary orders were active in Santo Domingo. Not until 1564 did the Vatican establish the archdiocese of Santo Domingo and confer upon its archbishop the title of Primate of the West Indies and of America. The authority of the archbishop unfortunately failed to live up to the illustriousness of his title, due to Santo Domingo's rapidly declining importance within the Spanish colonial system; nor has his stature been enhanced since independence, given the country's relatively minor position in Latin America. The colonial Church nonetheless managed to maintain a certain degree of prestige through the eminence of its university, which was considered to be the most venerable theological center in Spanish America.

The Church in the Dominican Republic lost a great deal of its power during the Haitian occupation. Perceiving the Church as an instrument of colonialism and slavery, the Haitians stripped it of all material assets. Even after independence, it failed to regain its former position. Over the next century, the Church struggled unsuccessfully to regain the right to property ownership, as concessions were granted by one government only to be withdrawn by the following government.

In 1929 only Trujillo's intervention stopped the congress from liquidating all Church property after the Dominican supreme court ruled that the Church had no legal existence. Trujillo used the Church as one of his many instruments of power. Under his rule, the Church became one part of the controlling triumvirate, the other two parts being the armed forces and the oligarchy.

Believing that Spanish priests would be more theologically conservative and more likely to preach obedience to his rule, Trujillo persuaded the Vatican to send a large contingent of priests from Spain to the Dominican Republic. The alliance between the dictator and the Vatican was sealed with the concordat of 1954. It established Roman Catholicism as the official religion in the Dominican Republic.

The Church often turned a blind eye to Trujillo's abuses of power, with a single exception in 1960, when Church officials protested the mass arrests of government opponents. This so incensed Trujillo that he ordered a campaign of harassment against the Church. Only his assassination prevented his planned imprisonment of the Dominican bishops.

Since the end of the Trujillo dictatorship, the Church's political power has declined, primarily due to a policy of "benign neglect" between the government and the Church.

The Roman Catholic Church was the primary agent for disseminating Spanish culture in the Americas through its missionaries and teaching.

ROMAN CATHOLICISM

Although many Dominicans are not regular churchgoers, most still mark significant life events with religious ceremonies and regard the parish priest as an important figure in rural society.

Dominicans respect the advice of the clergy concerning religious matters, but not secular matters. Nevertheless, the parish priest is often the only person outside the kinship group in whom Dominicans trust and confide.

Despite its diminished political power, the Church carries a major responsibility for public health care and education. The Church manages hospitals, clinics, pharmacies, orphanages, and convalescent homes, as well as nursery schools, elementary and secondary schools,

The bones of Columbus rested in Santa María la Menor until the quincentenary in 1992, when they were removed to the Columbus Lighthouse.

colleges, vocational and technical institutes, teacher-training colleges, and seminaries.

Catholic bishops have been vocal in demanding government reform with respect to human rights and poverty alleviation. At the parish level, some priests have tried to develop Christian-base communities in order to help people to organize and work together.

PROTESTANTISM

The first Protestants came to the Dominican Republic as migrants from North America in the 1820s. Their numbers increased around the turn of the century with the immigration of West Indian laborers. The 1960s and 1970s saw a boom in Dominican Protestantism, as evangelical Protestants successfully proselytized in the rural parts of the country. The primary evangelical groups in the Dominican Republic are the Seventh Day Adventists, the Dominican Evangelical Church, and the Assemblies of God.

Evangelical Protestants emphasize biblical fundamentalism, personal and familial rejuvenation, and economic entrepreneurship. Because services are conducted in a more egalitarian fashion than they are in the hierarchical Roman Catholic Church, poor Dominicans are especially attracted to Protestantism. Evangelical Protestant services are relatively spontaneous, allowing people to talk, sing, or give testimony about their religious experiences.

Tensions have been building between the Catholic Church and evangelical Protestants in the Dominican Republic. Many evangelical Protestants blame the concordat with the Vatican for marginalizing their churches and ministers, because it grants the Catholic Church privileges not accorded to evangelical Protestant Churches.

Evangelical Protestantism has a following among Dominicans. Roughly 5 percent of the population has adopted this new version of Christianity. Nevertheless, this is a low number compared with other Latin American countries, where more people have been converted.

FOLK BELIEFS

Many Dominicans perceive good or bad omens in various occurrences in daily life. There are many omens to do with death. For example, the cooing of wild doves near a house means that someone will die soon in the neighborhood. If an owl screeches near a house or alights on the roof, it announces a death in the family. If all the hens cackle together, a death will occur in the family or in the neighbor's family. Also, a person should avoid sleeping with feet toward the front of the house; a person who does that will die.

Then there are omens to do with money. If a person dreams of excrement, he can expect to receive money. The same goes if the palm of his right hand itches. But if his left palm itches, a forgotten debt will have to be paid, or he will lose money.

Several signs are believed to bring misfortune. Spilling the oil when filling a lamp announces misfortune for the person who spills it. Opening an umbrella inside the house, and sweeping the house at night also cause misfortune.

At night, when a horse tires after covering a relatively short distance, it is a sign that a ghost has been riding behind the rider. The rider should stop as soon as he realizes what is happening, or the ghost will give him the sickness from which the ghost died. To drive the ghost away, the saddle should be reversed, placing its front toward the tail of the horse.

FOLK RELIGION

Approximately 1 million Dominicans of Haitian descent continue to speak Creole French and celebrate their ancestral voodoo ceremonies. In the Dominican Republic, followers of voodoo generally practice their religion in secret, because the Dominican government and the general population deride it as pagan and African.

While the Dominicans claim that only Haitians practice voodoo, many of them nevertheless believe in the magical powers of voodoo.

FOLK REMEDIES Many Dominicans seek advice from *curanderos* (cur-ahn-DAY-rohs), or healers, and *brujos* (BREW-hos), or witch doctors. A *curandero* will often consult the saints to ascertain which herbs, roots, and various home cures to employ in their healing arts. The powers of the *brujo* are slightly more dramatic, since he can drive out possessive spirits that sometimes seize an individual. Dominicans consider *brujos* and *curanderos* intermediaries to God.

Some Dominicans also use certain prayers almost as incantations. Among the campesinos and the urban lower class, people recite specific prayers—generally to Jesus, the Virgin Mary, or a saint—in supplication for protection against evil or sometimes as formulas to cure specific diseases. A person might know one or two such prayers, which he or she believes to be a very powerful defence against evil spirits or against failure in any undertaking. Many Dominicans carry a copy of a favorite prayer as an amulet.

Incantations that are believed to be endowed with healing powers are called *ensalmos* (ehn-SAL-mohs). Folk healers use *ensalmos* like prescriptions for diagnosed illnesses—there are specific *ensalmos* for specific maladies. If someone faints, for example, a folk healer may whisper one such incantation in the person's ear.

Voodoo combines African and Roman Catholic elements.

LANGUAGE

THE OVERWHELMING MAJORITY of Dominicans speak Spanish, the official language of the Dominican Republic. As inhabitants of the first Spanish colony in the Americas, Dominicans take pride in speaking a clear, almost classical Spanish, just as they pride themselves on having the purest Spanish traditions in all of Latin America.

Dominican Spanish closely resembles the Castilian Spanish spoken in most of Spain. Differences in pronunciation derive from differences in the way the language has evolved on either side of the Atlantic Ocean since colonial times. For example, the soft *c* sound and the *z* are pronounced as a soft *th* (as in think) in most of contemporary Spain, whereas Dominicans pronounce the soft *c* and the *z* as an *s*.

English has influenced the Dominican language to a certain degree, mainly through the preponderance of Dominicans with family members and friends in the United States. Dominicans living in the United States, especially the so-called Dom-Yorks in New York City, take pride in their bilingual abilities and in their knowledge of U.S. culture.

TAINO/ARAWAK INFLUENCES

The Spaniards adopted several Taino/Arawak words. Many of these were subsequently absorbed into English. Words such as cassava, potato, tobacco, hammock, hurricane, and canoe are derived from the classical Spanish phonetic spellings of the Taino/Arawak words *cazabe* (KAH-sah-bay), *patata* (pah-TAH-tah), *tabaco* (tah-BAH-koh), *hamaca* (AH-mah-kah), *huracán* (uhr-ah-KAHN), and *canoa* (kahn-OH-ah). The list testifies to the impact of Amerindian products on European culture. The Spaniards also adopted geographical names such as *cibao*, or plain, and *bani*, or abundance of water. The city Higüey was named for one of the Taino/Arawak regional groups in the southeast.

As in most of Latin America, Dominicans greet each other with a kiss on the cheek. Women kiss each other in greeting. Men, however, greet each other with a handshake, unless they are very close, in which case they might hug each other heartily. Among young Dominicans, influenced by U.S. culture, a fisted handshake is the common greeting.

Opposite: **Signboards color busy Duarte Street in Santo Domingo.**

THE CURSE OF COLUMBUS

In spite of the fact that Christopher Columbus is considered a national hero, Dominicans have for centuries considered the utterance of his name to be bad luck. Instead of actually speaking his name, many Dominicans insist on referring to him indirectly as "the Admiral" or "the Discoverer." One commits a *fucú* (foo-KU), or invites bad luck, by calling him by name. It is common to use his name as an all-purpose expletive. Dominicans exclaim "¡*Colón*!" (Columbus's Spanish name) much in the same fashion that they might cry out "¡*Ay, Dios*!"

Propaganda for the quincentenary, or 500th anniversary celebration of Columbus's arrival in the Americas, tried with limited success to drown out the superstition regarding the explorer's name. When the Columbus Lighthouse was finally turned on, many Dominicans prayed that they would not be cursed; some government officials even refused to attend the lighthouse's

inauguration. It has been said that the *fucú* cursed aspects of the lighthouse construction, including the crashing in 1937 of three airplanes—named for Columbus's ships the *Niña*, the *Pinta*, and the *Santa María*—in a fundraising flight for the lighthouse.

There are many more bizarre incidents that have served to convince Dominicans of all classes that the *fucú* is legitimate. In the 1940s a politician was pricked by a medal when he was awarded the Order of Columbus; the politician died when the wound became infected. In 1946, at a ceremony marking the 450th anniversary of Santo Domingo's founding, an earthquake struck when Columbus's urn was opened.

AFRICAN INFLUENCES

One of the oldest and most pervasive elements of Dominican culture is the concept of the *fucú*. African slaves brought the word with them to the island, although its exact origin in Africa is unknown.

A *fucú* is something of ill omen that is likely to bring bad luck; it can also describe something of doom in a person, a place, or an event. At the materialization of a *fucú* in any form, Dominicans will sign a cross in the air with their index fingers and exclaim "*Zafa!*" (SAH-fah)—a verbal remedy to any curse the *fucú* might inflict upon them. The word *zafa* was also introduced by African slaves.

RIDDLES

Although declining in frequency, riddling still constitutes an enjoyable pastime in the smaller towns and rural areas of the Dominican Republic. When campesinos gather for wakes, weddings, or other social occasions, they may start telling riddles after exhausting the various topics of conversation. Someone starts the process by offering the first riddle to the group, in a playfully challenging attitude. The group responds with a great deal of comment and criticism before answering or, if it is a new riddle unknown to them, giving up. After that, everyone comments on the riddle again and jokes about it in light of its interpretation. Then someone else follows up with perhaps another riddle with the same answer, or with a new and different riddle.

In spite of attempts by the government and the military to intimidate the media in the Dominican Republic, it remains one of the freest in all Latin America.

The content of many of the riddles concern everyday objects, such as avocados, honey bees, needles, or garlic. Some riddles suggest sexual concepts either obliquely or overtly. Riddles that merely suggest sexual ideas but then give inoffensive answers may be recited in front of women, but it is considered improper for women to recite them.

The riddle is distinguished by how eloquently the speaker poses it, so that it works not only as a puzzle to be solved, but also so that it has artistic merit. Sometimes the riddles are offered in poetic verse.

Riddle:	*White I leave my house.*		Riddle:	*The one who makes it does not use it.*
	Green was my birth.			*The one who uses it does not see it.*
	With the maturation of time			*The one who sees it does not desire it*
	White I return to my house.			*no matter how pretty it may be.*
Answer: Garlic			Answer:	A coffin

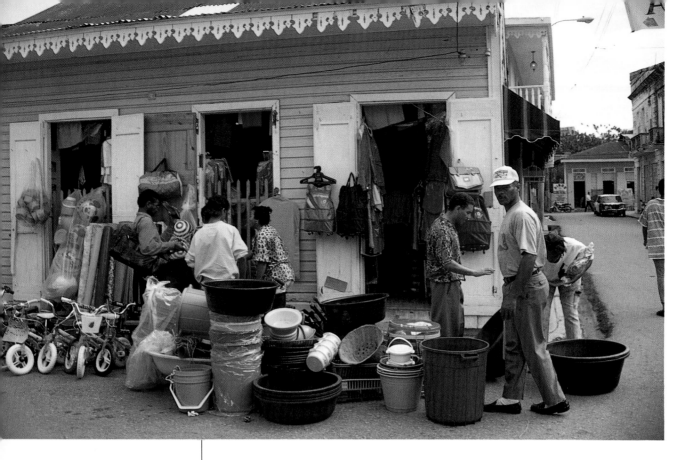

Bartering is a natural part of life among neighbors, and they like nothing more than negotiating a good deal.

DOMINICAN SAYINGS AND EXPRESSIONS

Dominicans demonstrate their renowned friendliness with a gracious welcome to anyone who enters their home. Visitors are greeted with the traditional expression "*Mi casa, su casa*" (mee kah-sah, soo kah-sah), meaning my house is your house.

Several sayings and expressions, or *dichos* (DEE-chohs), describe the relation of skin color to class and political power. Examples are "colonels are never black" (even if their skin is dark), "money whitens," and "a rich black is a mulatto, a rich mulatto is a white man." However, Dominicans also make light of their color-consciousness, with *dichos* such as "we all have a little black behind the ears."

Some Dominican sayings derive from a Spanish heritage. For example, "no Moors on the coast" means figuratively "the coast is clear." The expression refers to the centuries-long war between medieval Spain and the Islamic Moors, and it also suggests the Dominican resentment of Haiti's occupation in the 19th century. Another Spanish saying that is also common in the Dominican Republic is "the Devil is wise more because he is old than because he is the Devil," signifying that wisdom comes with age or experience.

Certain proverbs and sayings carry the flavor of their rural origins. "While the dog is skinniest, he has the most fleas" signifies that misfortune continues to plague the person who is already suffering. Another folk saying, "one can always find a hair in the *sancocho* (san-KOH-choh)," or stew, means that good things are never perfect. The pragmatic nature of the Dominican campesino is demonstrated by the proverb "better to say 'from here I fled' than 'here I died.'"

BASIC DOMINICAN PRONUNCIATION

a	*a* as in cart	*h*	silent
e	*e* as in they or *a* as in day	*j*	*h* as in hat
i	*ee* as in meet	*l*	*l* as in ball
o	*o* as in note	*ll*	*y* as in yes
u	*oo* as in boot or *u* as in flute	*m*	*m* as in map
y	*ee* as in meet or *j* as in jar	*n*	*n* as in noon
b	*b* as in boy	*ñ*	*ny* as in canyon
c	*k* as in kind; or *s* as in sit, when before *e* or *i*	*p*	*p* as in purse
		q	*k* as in kind
ch	*ch* as in child	*r*	rolled, especially if first letter
d	*d* as in dog; resembles *th* as in they when at the end of a word	*rr*	strongly rolled
		s	*s* as in sit
f	*f* as in off	*t*	*t* as in tilt
g	*g* as in go; a guttural *ch* as in the Scottish word loch, when before *e* or *i*	*v*	*b* as in boy
		x	*x* as in exit
		z	*s* as in sit

ARTS

DOMINICANS PRIZE artistic endeavors of all kinds, but their country is primarily recognized for its music and dance. Dominicans seem to live and breathe the merengue, a style of music and dance that originated on the island of Hispaniola.

Originally a rural folk dance and later a ballroom dance, the merengue is danced with a limping step, the weight always on the same foot. It is said to have been first danced by a crippled general whose guests respectfully imitated his movements as he dragged his lame right leg across the floor. Both the music and the dance are extremely popular throughout Latin America and with Hispanics in the United States.

The Dominican Republic has a relatively strong literary tradition, although it is not as widely recognized outside the country. The literary arts have been dominated by writers from powerful families, many of whom combined their literary talents with political careers.

With the loss of the Taino Arawak influence, Dominican arts developed out of the Hispanic and African origins of the Dominican people. The Hispanic influence dominates the literary arts; the African influence is most evident in Dominican music, especially popular music.

Opposite: **A mural on a university building in Santo Domingo.**

Below: **Brightly colored folk paintings for sale.**

LITERARY ARTS

The most significant writer of the colonial period was Bartolomé de Las Casas. Las Casas recorded the early history of the Caribbean area in his *Historía de las Indias*, which remains one of the most important historical records of the Spanish conquest of the Americas and the indigenous peoples of the Caribbean.

Dominican literature developed during the Romantic era in France, and that style's influence persisted in the Dominican Republic through the 19th century. The outstanding work of that period was the classic Dominican novel *Enriquillo*, published in 1882, by Manuel de Jesús Galván (1834–1910). Exemplifying the Romantic ideal of "the noble savage," *Enriquillo* stands out as a masterpiece of Spanish-American literature. In 1954 Robert Graves translated Galván's novel into English with the title *The Cross and the Sword*.

A leading contemporary of Galván was Salomé Ureña de Henríquez (1850–96), a schoolteacher who wrote poetry filled with patriotic fervor about political themes of the day. Much of her poetry was intensely personal in style.

A guilty nostalgia for the vanished Taino Arawak characterizes Dominican literary works of the Romantic period, called the *indigenismo* (een-dee-hay-NEES-moh) literary movement.

Literary arts

The evolution from romanticism to realism and then to modernism took only a decade in the Dominican Republic. Gastón Fernando Deligne (1861–1912) led the modernist movement. Inspired by Nicaragua's Rubén Darío, Deligne aspired to modernist symbolism, declaring that "to write poetry is to turn ideas into images."

Another literary movement of the early 20th century was *postumismo* (pohs-too-MEES-moh), which attempted to establish a new style of poetry and prose by casting off Spanish and early Dominican influences. Domingo Moreno Jimenes (1894–1986) exemplifies *postumismo* in his work *Palabras en el Agua* (*Words on Water*). The poetry presents images floating and jostling each other in the current of incessant change.

A recent literary movement, *poesía de sorpresa* (poh-AYS-EEYA day sor-PRAY-sah), or surprise poetry, has developed out of the *postumismo* movement. *Poesía de sorpresa* utilizes imagery deliberately chosen for its shock effect. Héctor Incháustegui Cabral (1912–79) led the *poesía de sorpresa* movement with works such as *El Miedo en un Puñado de Polvo* (*Fear in a Handful of Dust*). This dramatic trilogy in verse draws its themes from Greek tragedy and its style from T.S. Eliot.

Former president Bosch is also known for several novels and short stories, the best of which are collected in two volumes of short stories, *Cuentos Escritos en el Exilio* (*Stories Written in Exile*) and *Más Cuentos Escritos en el Exilio* (*More Stories Written in Exile*). He has also written several political polemics, as well as a history of his aborted presidency, *Crisis of Democracy of America in the Dominican Republic*.

Contemporary poet and novelist Julia Alvarez writes about modern life for the large group of Dom-Yorks who live between two cultures, U.S. and Dominican. Her novel *In the Time of the Butterflies* (1995), about repression under the Trujillo dictatorship, was made into a film starring Salma Hayek in 2001.

Enriquillo *is named for one of the last Taino Arawak caciques, Enrique, who had been educated and brought up as a Christian by the Spaniards but rebelled in 1533 after being enslaved with his wife. He escaped with a few hundred remaining Taino Arawak to the Sierra de Bahoruco, and finally surrendered to the Spanish forces on an island in the middle of the salt lake that still bears his name.*

Traditional dances are
relived at festival time.

MUSIC

The most famous kind of Dominican music and dance is the merengue, which Dominicans share with Haitians. The merengue combines the Spanish *pasodoble* (pah-soh-DOH-blay), or two-step, with the African tom-tom. Couples dance, in casual or traditional dress, with limping steps to rhythmic lyrics that comment on love, politics, destiny, or even illegal emigration to the United States.

Campesinos from the Cibao developed the merengue and turned it into a national obsession. In the city, the merengue music gushes from taxis, self-service stores, bars, restaurants, and even fast-food outlets. Merengue serves as the background music for everyday Dominican life. In the evening, it turns the waterfront of Santo Domingo into an open-air gala, warmly pulsating with noise, music, people, lights, and cars.

A special merengue festival takes place in Santo Domingo in the last week of July. All along the waterfront, Dominicans and thousands of tourists from Puerto Rico and Western Europe celebrate the merengue with all-night partying.

The guitar is probably the most popular musical instrument in the Dominican Republic. In some rural areas, musicians also commonly play flutes and homemade marimbas. Merengue music is played on locally made percussion instruments, such as the *tambora* (tahm-BOH-rah) and the *guiro* (goo-EER-oh), although high-tech synthesizers are sometimes used instead. By rubbing the *guiro* with a shell or with wire, the musician produces the rasping noise behind the merengue rhythm.

Spanish bolero music and dance are quite popular in the Dominican Republic, as is salsa music. If the merengue expresses the natural vivacity of Dominicans, their pathos is expressed through mournfully romantic *bachata* (bah-chah-tah) ballads. Young Dominicans also enjoy reggae and other modern African-American music, as well as rock music.

The guitar is widely used in Dominican music.

Some regions have preserved folkloric dances that are more heavily European in style. In the south, the *mangulina* (mahn-goo-LEE-nah) is commemorated at patron saints' day festivals, as is *la jacana* (la ha-KAH-nah) in the north. These types of ceremonial dances, with Spanish and Taino Arawak origins, form part of the Dominican Republic's folkloric tradition but are not part of the popular culture. Another type of music derived from Spain, which has been preserved in the northern region, consists of ancient vocal choruses known as *salves* (SAHL-vays) and *tonadas* (toh-NAH-dahs).

Dominican composers did without established orchestras until Trujillo created the National Conservatory of Music and Speech in 1941. That year Dominican composers created 20 important musical works.

AN INVOLVED ART

As with most Caribbean forms of live music and dance performances, the merengue depends upon collective participation. There is no division between active performers and a passive audience. While certain gifted instrumentalists or singers might dominate certain segments of the performance, members of the audience are expected to participate by clapping, offering encouragement, or even dancing themselves. In fact, the more enthusiastically the audience participates, the more successful the performance becomes. The exchange develops into a circular process, in which the leading musicians and singers are spurred on to greater degrees of musical execution by higher and higher levels of audience participation.

Merengue lyrics are noted for their use of social commentary on love and politics. They are often ironic, humorous, or critical, skillfully using sexual double entendres and provocative allusions. Others comment on issues of everyday life. A contemporary merengue song, by Wilfredo Vargas (Karen Records), says:

*"Puerto Rico queda cerca, pero móntate en avión,
y si consigues la visa, no hay problema en Inmigración.
Pero no te vayas en yola, no te llenes de ilusiones,
porque en el Canal de la Mona, te comen los tiburones."*

"Puerto Rico is close by, but get yourself on a plane,
and if you can get a visa, no problem in immigration.
But don't you go by *yola*, don't let your dreams delude you,
because in the Mona Passage, the sharks will surely eat you."

PAINTING

Painters in the Dominican Republic have not developed a uniquely Dominican style, although the country has produced many fine painters. Several have achieved notice in Europe and the United States, including Guillo Pérez, Gilberto Hernández Ortega, Ada Balcácer, and Abelardo Urdaneta. While they portray common Dominican themes, they generally do not share a distinctly Dominican mode of expression.

The most prominent style of Dominican painting during the 20th century was *costumbrismo* (kohs-toom-BREES-moh), which portrays Dominican customs and themes. Urdaneta was a precursor of *costumbrismo*, while Pérez has continued to develop it within a realistic style. Pérez was famous for portraying sugarcane fields and oxen driven along rutted wagon trails. Later in his career, and in keeping with his reputation for masterful use of color, he concentrated on depicting roosters.

The foremost contemporary Dominican painter is the master Ramón Oviedo. His work over the last 40 years has documented Dominican life and politics, and he has exhibited his work worldwide.

The bright colors and expressionist style of Haitian paintings *(top)* contrast with Dominican art.

FOLK ARTS AND CRAFTS

Dominican arts and crafts have recently experienced a resurgence throughout the country. The renewed interest is partly due to a collective search for cultural roots among modern-day Dominicans and partly due to encouragement from the government and international development agencies, which see the crafts as a beneficial means of lowering the unemployment rate. Women artisans especially have gained prominence in the revival of traditional Dominican crafts.

Campesinos in the Cibao region carefully preserve a rich tradition of pottery for household use and a creative art. Decorative ceramics include the production of lamp bases, vases, ashtrays, nativity scenes, ornamental plates, candle holders, and dolls.

NATIONAL JEWELS

Amber and larimar are extremely popular materials, especially in the making of jewelry. Early humans believed that amber captured the sun's rays, and it has been prized for centuries for its beauty and ease of carving.

Amber is a translucent fossil formed from pine tree sap that hardened over millions of years under the weight of layers of soil and ice. Sometimes, the sap trapped organic materials, such as insects, lizards, and flowers, perfectly preserving its silent victims. Clear amber is popular in jewelry, but scientists greatly value amber with imprisoned fossils, from which they can retrieve DNA material. In 1989 a piece of Dominican amber conclusively proved that mushrooms were 40 million years old, twice as old as previously believed.

The Baltic region traditionally has been the world's primary source of amber, but the Dominican Republic holds some of the largest reserves in the world (at an estimated age of 20 to 40 million years), as well as some of the most colorful specimens of the gem. Although primarily yellow, orange, or brown, Dominican amber also comes in red, green, blue, and even purple.

Found only in the Dominican Republic, larimar is a semiprecious Dominican stone that is unique because its blue tones vary from deep sky blue to blue green—the result of contact with copper and cobalt oxide during its geological formation. When the larimar deposits on the southern coast were first discovered in 1974, Dominicans believed that the stone came from the sea. In actuality, the rivers washed the stones down from the mountain tops and deposited them near the ocean to be naturally polished by the water. One of the first commercial suppliers of the gem named it after his daughter Lari and the sea, *el mar* (ehl mahr). Today, miners excavate the stone by hand in open pits near Sierra de Bahoruco.

Other popular crafts include palm weaving, woodcarving, leatherwork, doll making, and jewelry making. Weavers in various parts of the country use local fibers, including various types of palm leaves, to make baskets, hats, hammock ties, and floor mats and rugs. Artisans also craft popular jewelry from amber, larimar, seashells, tortoiseshell, bone, and coral.

The community of Salcedo produces decoratively carved products from *higuero* (ee-GOOAIR-oh), or calabash, such as lacquered purses, rounded mulatto faces, fish, Spanish maracas, and *guiros*, a merengue instrument. *Guiros* are elongated calabash gourds that the artisan dries and empties through a small hole before carving transverse grooves on the shell. Maracas, used to accompany Spanish music, are dried and hollowed gourds with numerous small seeds inside that make a rasping sound when the gourds are shaken.

LEISURE

DOMINICANS ARE AMONG the most cheerful people in the world. They face their difficulties with resignation and overlook them in order to celebrate life, family, and friendship as best they can. Since most Dominicans work at least six days a week, they have little time for recreation. Social life in small towns centers around the central plaza, and men also gather to gossip in the bars and poolrooms; in the rural neighborhoods, or *aldeas* (ahl-DAY-ahs), people congregate at the *colmado* (kohl-MAH-doh), or store.

Sunday remains the only day of leisure for most people. Farm families often come to town on Sundays to shop or go to church. After church, people gather in the town plaza and visit with friends. The women and children usually return home early to prepare dinner, while the men stay and chat, enjoy a cockfight, or watch a baseball or volleyball game.

Small towns are usually quiet places. If someone manages to buy a television, the neighbors will gather at his house in the evenings. Most shows are imported from Mexico, Puerto Rico, or the United States. Whether or not they find the programs interesting, people find plenty to exclaim over in the clothes, the food, the cars, and the commercials.

Opposite: **Dominicans enjoy sailing on a sunny day.**

Below: **Men gather to gossip in a typical bar in Santo Domingo.**

Volleyball is popular with Dominican children.

SPORTS

The most popular team sports in the Dominican Republic are baseball, soccer, volleyball, and basketball. Soccer's following in the country, though active, is small in relation to that in most of Latin America, but baseball is the national passion of the Dominican Republic, fueled by competition in the Caribbean and close contact with North American professional teams.

In 1974 Santo Domingo hosted the Twelfth Central American and Caribbean Olympic Games, in which approximately 4,000 athletes participated. For the event, the Dominican government constructed an array of facilities, including a large sports palace with a seating capacity of 10,000 spectators, an Olympic-sized swimming pool, a bicycle track, and a shooting range.

BASEBALL Among organized sports, baseball inspires the most national enthusiasm. The Dominican Republic exports more professional baseball

players to the United States than does any other country, while major league players from the United States often spend their winters in the Dominican Republic, playing in the professional leagues there. The baseball season begins after the World Series in the United States and runs from October through January.

Dominicans start playing baseball almost as soon as they can walk, practicing with old broomsticks and hollowed-out coconut husks for bases. They share gloves and bats between teams, but always play with the high-level intensity that characterizes Dominican baseball. They concentrate on simply throwing, hitting, and running, without coaches, uniforms, or warm-ups. Men continue to play either among themselves or on organized amateur teams. Those who show talent can reasonably hope that they will be drafted by a professional team in the Caribbean, Canada, or the United States.

It was the Cubans, rather than the U.S. Marines as many people believe, who brought baseball to the Dominican Republic. The Cubans

Although Trujillo was not a big fan of baseball himself, he aggressively promoted the sport and Dominican participation in international competition in order to enhance his own reputation.

DOMINICAN BASEBALL PLAYERS IN THE UNITED STATES

Ozzie Virgil was the first Dominican to move to North America to play baseball professionally in the 1950s. Brothers Jesús, Felipe, and Matty Alou were among the most successful Dominican baseball players in the 1980s. Juan Marichal played for the San Francisco Giants and became the first Dominican in the Baseball Hall of Fame. Other famous Dominican players include Juan Samuel, José Rijo, Tony Peña, Pedro Guerrero, Tony Fernández, George Bell, and Alex Rodríguez. Sammy Sosa, who played for the Chicago Cubs for most of his career, became a superstar in the 1998 Major League season after hitting 66 home runs, the most by any Latin American. In 2003 he made history again as the first Latin American to hit 500 career home runs. Pedro Martínez and Manny Ramírez were the star pitcher and left fielder of the Boston Red Sox in the team's game against the Saint Louis Cardinals in the 2004 World Series final, which the Red Sox won—their first World Series victory in 86 years.

"If you ask any Dominican what he is proudest of, he will read you a list of ball-players. This country doesn't have much, but we know we are the best in the world at one thing. That's not bragging, because it's true. And we plan to continue being the best in the world at it."

—Manuel Mota, former outfielder for the Los Angeles Dodgers

learned the game from U.S. troops stationed in Cuba in the 1860s. The fact that baseball originated in the United States did influence its popularity, however. Starting out as an amateur sport, the game was organized professionally in the 1920s and 1930s, during which time Dominican players gained international recognition for their talent and skill. Furthermore, several legendary U.S. baseball players, including Satchel Paige, were lured away from the segregated Negro League to play for Dominican teams in the heated season of 1937.

Dominican baseball declined after that, though it maintained an avid following at the amateur level, bolstered by play in the sugarcane fields during the slack harvest period. Plantation and refinery managers and owners encouraged employees to play as a diversion in slow times. The game developed a distinctly Dominican flavor, characterized by a close-knit bond between players and their passionate fans.

Professional baseball reemerged in the Dominican Republic during the 1950s, and U.S. teams began recruiting Dominicans. Amateur play had matured to such an extent that professional teams could draw from amateur teams.

By the 1980s there were hundreds of Dominican baseball players in North America. Their successes encouraged the signing of more professional contracts for Dominicans, who contributed to baseball history in the United States into the 21st century.

Cockfighting fans get passionate about the matches, primarily because of the heavy gambling before and during a match.

COCKFIGHTING

Many Dominican men, especially in the rural areas, remain enthusiastic about cockfighting, although the authorities have tried to suppress interest in this brutal spectator sport. Introduced by the Spaniards, it often provokes criticism from foreign visitors, who charge that it is inherently cruel to the birds. Before the U.S. occupation in 1916, cockfighting was the national pastime, but it has given way to baseball.

Popularized in ancient Rome, cockfighting is an amateur sporting event in which the owners of gamecocks, or *gallos* (GAH-yohs), put their birds in a circular ring about 20 feet (6.1 m) in diameter and let them fight, sometimes to the death. The owners breed and train their gallos especially for fighting, which the birds begin between ages 1 and 2. The birds are equipped with metal or bone spurs averaging about 1.5 inches (3.8 cm) in length, to enhance their ability to hurt their opponents.

After fitting the artificial spurs over the gamecocks' natural spurs, the handlers put the birds into the ring at the same time. The birds become infuriated at the proximity of the other bird or birds and will run and jump at them, trying to spur and wound them in the eyes or chest. On occasion, if one of the birds refuses to fight any longer, the handler will put it breast to breast with the other bird. If the *gallo* still refuses to fight, the judge will rule that it has quit, and the fight ends.

Lapén *(lah-PAIN)*
is a Spanish
approximation
of the French
word for rabbit,
although most
campesinos do
not regard the
Lapén tales as
animal stories.
Just as slaves in
the United States
used to tell stories
about Brer Rabbit,
the campesinos
see Lapén and the
other characters as
characterizations
of themselves.

URBAN NIGHTLIFE

Santo Domingo comes alive at night. The middle and upper classes dress up elegantly—women elaborately made-up in dresses and high-heels, and men in ties, slicked-back hair, and cologne. They throng to the city's many restaurants, nightclubs, and casinos, where they eat, drink, and dance to merengue and salsa music until the early hours of the morning.

Since many people cannot afford to enter the expensive nightclubs, however, it is becoming increasingly common for individuals to set up their stereos and large speakers on the sidewalks of the city, creating an atmosphere of cacophonous partying. In the evening, Santo Domingo's waterfront, the Malecón, is transformed into a narrow, 3-mile-long (5-km-long) street party, filled with cars, pedestrians, dancers, music, and jubilant noise.

THE TALE OF GODFATHER DEATH

A laborer's eighth child had not been baptized because no godfather had been found. He passed over Christ and chose the devil as the godfather. The devil gave his adopted son the powers of healing through an herb. However, the devil warned his godson that if he saw the devil standing at the foot of the bed, any attempt at healing the patient would be futile.

The king fell very ill and offered the hand of his daughter, the princess, in marriage to anyone who could cure him. When the healer arrived, he was surprised to see his godfather, the devil, standing at the foot of the bed. In spite of the devil's warning, he commanded four maids to pick up the bed and turn it around; thus he healed the king and won the hand of the princess. Just before the wedding, the devil called his godson into his cave and revealed to him that the "lamp of life" showed that he was to live only a short time longer. The boy died before leaving the cave.

Opposite: **Young Dominicans enjoy** *marimba* **dancing at a street party.**

Below: **Dominicans meet in the park on Sunday to talk and tell stories.**

ORAL TRADITION

With increasing access to television, storytelling and listening to riddles are no longer as popular with Dominicans as in the not-too-distant past. Today the pastimes of storytelling and riddling exist primarily in small towns or on farms, providing entertainment during social gatherings such as wakes or weddings, during the midday siesta, on Sunday afternoons in the park, or while visiting someone's home.

A relatively large body of folktales exists in the Dominican Republic. Most of the tales have European origins, but a few have African parallels. A set of folktales concern the adventures of Juan Bobo, and another cycle of tales involves Buquí and Lapén. Common folktale themes include magical flights, monsters, supernatural beings, and tales of heroism, morality, trickery, and enchantment.

FESTIVALS

DOMINICANS ARE in general a people who love to celebrate. They love to dance, go to parties, and eat and drink heartily. Many take advantage of the weekends to have a good time, but holidays are celebrated with special enthusiasm.

Carnival is the high point of the year. In the Dominican Republic, Carnival coincides with Independence Day celebrations, giving the holiday added significance.

Dominicans celebrate Christmas throughout the month of December, ending on Three Kings' Day on January 6. Easter may be celebrated religiously or used as an excuse for a trip to the beach.

CALENDAR OF EVENTS	
January 1	New Year's Day
January 6	Epiphany
January 21	Our Lady of Altagracia
January 26	Duarte's Birthday
February 27	Independence Day
Variable	Carnival
Variable	Good Friday
May 1	Labor Day
Variable	Corpus Christi
August 16	Restoration Day
September 24	Our Lady of las Mercedes
November 6	Constitution Day
December 25	Christmas Day

Opposite: **Dance is an integral part of Dominican celebrations.**

THE CHRISTMAS SEASON

Dominicans celebrate Christmas throughout the month of December. They have parties every weekend with family, coworkers, and friends. Dominicans who live abroad flock back to their pueblos, or villages, bearing exotic gifts. Real Christmas trees have become more common in recent years, but traditional Dominican Christmas "trees" are really branches. People might paint the branches white or green and then decorate them with miniature straw or ceramic crafts shaped as hats, baskets, angels, and other objects.

On Christmas Eve, the Dominican extended family enjoys a feast of roasted pig. Catholics then attend a midnight Mass. The church is decorated with a *nacimiento* (nah-see-mee-AIN-toh), or nativity scene, with life-sized wooden images of Joseph, the Virgin Mary, and *el Niño Jesús*, or the Baby Jesus, surrounded by horses, sheep, cows, and shepherds. After the Mass, many people return home to party until sunrise, while teenagers and couples go out dancing. On Christmas day, *el Niño Jesús* bears gifts to children in the Cibao region, while children in Santo Domingo receive gifts from Santa Claus.

The Christmas season ends with the arrival of the Three Kings on January 6. It is considered a day for children, who sometimes receive additional holiday gifts from visiting relatives.

EASTER

Dominicans no longer celebrate Easter as religiously as in the past. Nevertheless, for religious Catholics, Semana Santa and Easter Sunday are highly ritualistic holidays. In Santo Domingo, parishioners take the wooden images of Jesus Christ from the churches and march through the streets with the images at the head of the procession.

Dominicans used to believe that if a person went to the beach at Easter, they would turn into a fish. Now, Easter is considered the perfect time for a beach holiday.

QUINCENTENARY

Dominican leaders spent more than a century planning for the 500th anniversary of Columbus's arrival in the Americas, which was celebrated on Columbus Day, October 12, 1992. The most significant part of the celebration was the Faro a Colón, or Columbus Lighthouse, the construction of which was first discussed in the mid-1800s. Ground was broken under Trujillo in 1948, however, the actual construction did not begin until 1986.

The design for the Columbus Lighthouse was chosen through an architectural contest in 1931.

The monument is a long horizontal cross, half a mile (0.8 km) long, with slanting walls 120 feet (36.6 m) high. The lighthouse throws a cross of light against the sky rather than across the sea. When lit, its 30 billion-candlepower beacon is visible from Puerto Rico, 150 miles (241.4 km) east.

The construction of the Faro a Colón cost an estimated $70 million dollars, although the government insists it cost only $11 million. The expense of building and powering the memorial has caused a great deal of controversy and resentment among Dominicans.

Unfortunately for the organizers of the celebration, the quincentennial anniversary became the target of transatlantic controversy over the legacy of Columbus. Indigenous peoples in the Americas protested that his "discovery" of the Americas resulted in the destruction of whole civilizations; others celebrated the profound ramifications of this unprecedented exchange of cultures, cuisines, technology, and medical knowledge.

The *diablo cojuelo* of La Vega are the most anthropomorphic, with threatening or mocking expressions less common in other cities. In Santo Domingo masks have horns and exaggerated mouths ranging from thick lips to piranha jaws or duck bills. In Santiago masks are decorated with shells or jewels and have remarkably detailed horns. In Monte Cristi headpieces represent bulls.

CARNIVAL AND INDEPENDENCE DAY

Carnival originated in medieval Europe as the final feasting and merry-making before Lent, the 40 days of fasting and penitence that precede Good Friday and Easter. The Dominican Republic's Independence Day always falls close to the beginning of Lent so that independence and Carnival celebrations often coincide on February 27.

African influences embellish Dominican Carnival celebrations, which resemble Carnival celebrations in Rio de Janeiro and New Orleans. Dominicans dress in a colorful array of fantastic masks and costumes, including European and African designs. One Carnival character is the *diablo cojuelo* (dee-AHB-loh kohn-HOOAY-loh), a horned devil that lashes out at bystanders with inflated cow bladders to purge them of sin. Anthropologists from the Museo del Hombre Dominicano in Santo Domingo have traced the *diablo cojuelo* to medieval Europe.

Street parties some-
times include a beauty
pageant.

Other Carnival characters include *Roba la Gallina* (ROH-bah la gah-YEE-nah), who dresses as a transvestite and attracts chanting verses from the spectators; *Marimanta* (mah-ree-MAHN-tah), represented by women in white twirling wide skirts; and *la Muerte Enjipe* (lah MOOAIR-tay ain-HEE-pay), men in black suits with painted skeletons, who dance around the *Marimanta*. They form part of a parade of floats and outlandishly costumed marchers from various municipalities, businesses, and clubs. The parade begins in the late afternoon on Independence Day, when the newly elected king and queen of the celebrations arrive on the Malecón, Santo Domingo's waterfront.

Hundreds of wooden stalls called *casetas* (cah-SAY-tahs) are set up along the Malecón, selling rum, sodas, beer, sandwiches, fruit, and other snacks. Each *caseta* plays merengue music on its own radio. Hundreds of thousands of spectators line the Malecón during the parade, and the celebration continues all night long with dancing, singing, and partying in the street.

FOOD

THE DOMINICAN DIET includes a lot of starch, such as rice, tubers, and plantains, in place of meat. Many Dominicans derive most of their protein from beans, a complete protein when combined with rice. Another common source of vegetable protein is pigeon peas, called *guandules* (guan-DOO-lays) in the Dominican Republic, which are often substituted for beans and served with rice. Rich or poor, Dominicans love to eat; food is an important part of celebrations, holidays, and any occasion where people get together.

Above: **Beans for sale in the market. Beans are the main ingredient in Dominican cooking.**

Opposite: **A vendor sells fresh fruit at a market in the Dominican Republic.**

ORIGINS OF CARIBBEAN CUISINE

The colonization of the Americas brought about a global food exchange that permanently influenced cuisines all over the world. The colonists incorporated into their own diet cassava, sweet potatoes, annatto and allspice, hot peppers, and various kinds of beans and fruit from the Caribbean, as well as tomatoes, potatoes, peanuts, papayas, cacao, and avocados from continental America.

In turn, the colonists brought a wide range of foods from elsewhere in the world: from Europe, vegetables such as onions, leeks, carrots, cabbages, asparagus, and artichokes, which flourished in the Caribbean climate; from Africa, millet, okra, watermelons, ackee, plantains, and bananas; from Oceania, mangoes, taro, and breadfruit; and from India and Indonesia, spices.

Through the centuries of exchange and adaptation, Caribbean cuisine developed its own distinctive character. Rather than percolating from the upper-class diet downward to the campesinos, Caribbean cuisine came from the choicest dishes of the poor to become the colorful diet of the elite.

ESSENTIAL INGREDIENTS

Dominican food is described as *comida criolla* (koh-MEE-dah kree-OH-yah), or creole food. It consists primarily of white rice, black or red beans, plantains, and occasionally meat in the form of pork, goat, or, less often, beef. Dominicans like their food spicy but not excessively hot.

Plantains are popular because they are sweet, plentiful, and cheap. Although they resemble the banana, they are larger, more angular, have thicker skins, and must be cooked before eating. Whereas the banana is high in sugar and low in starch, plantains are high in starch and low in sugar. Similar to a potato in texture, plantains are often sliced and fried. Green plantains may be fried, pounded flat, then refried and seasoned with garlic to make *tostones* (tohs-TOHN-ays), or they may be mashed and fried with onions to make the common breakfast dish *mangu* (MAHN-goo). Cassava, sweet potatoes, taro, and yams, which are cheap and easy to grow, also form part of the campesino diet.

A particular Dominican specialty is *sancocho*, a stew made of chicken or some other meat, cooked with cassava and plantains, and seasoned with pepper, coriander, and a dash of vinegar. *Mondongo* (mohn-DOHN-goh), also popular, is made with tripe.

Dominicans who can afford it enjoy dishes made with pork or goat. Deep-fried pork or chicken skins are also popular, as are various types of sausage made from beef or pork.

Seafood is plentiful in most parts of the country, but some common species, such as red snapper and grouper, are occasionally toxic. Shark, tuna, salmon, cod, lobster, and shellfish are popular. In Samaná, people like to sweeten seafood with coconut.

BEVERAGES Dominicans drink a wide variety of fruit juices, made from the island's abundant fruit, including tamarindo, níspero, jauga, guava, soursop, pineapple, mango, orange, grapefruit, and papaya. They mix the freshly squeezed juice with ice to make *jugo* (HOO-goh) or whisk the juice with milk and ice to make *batido* (bah-TEE-doh).

Dominicans drink coffee at least three times a day with meals. They might buy juice or coffee from restaurants or street vendors throughout the day.

Dominicans enjoy drinking beer and rum in the evenings and on weekends. These are also the most popular alcoholic beverages during holidays or ceremonial celebrations such as weddings.

Above: **Poor campesinos often depend almost solely on plantains, which they eat boiled, with noodles and broth.**

Opposite: **Beans and rice are the basic ingredients in the national dish, called *arroz con habichuelas* (ahrr-OHS kohn ah-bee-choo-AY-lahs) when cooked separately, or *moro* when cooked together.**

MEALTIMES

Dominican families eat most of their meals together, even the midday meal, unless one or both parents cannot return from work. The mother often serves everyone at the table, especially in rural families where she wants to make sure that everyone receives a fair portion. In rural households, children generally do not serve themselves at mealtimes. The mother does the serving, and they must clean their plates. In many urban families, however, everyone at the table serves themselves.

BREAKFAST The first meal of the day, *el desayuno* (el day-sai-OON-oh), usually consists of plantains or some type of boiled root, especially in the rural areas, where campesinos need a filling breakfast to start off the day. In the cities, *el desayuno* may consist of cereal or bread with coffee and juice.

Men selling rice and beans in the market.

LUNCH Lunch is the largest meal of the day and is often followed by a siesta, or rest period. Lunch, or *el almuerzo* (al-moo-AIR-soh), always consists of rice and beans in some form, and may include meat, or perhaps the stew *sancocho*.

Dominicans try to eat *el almuerzo* at home if possible, although many workers must take their lunches to work with them and do not take a siesta. In small towns, all businesses close for a few hours in the middle of the day and open again in the afternoon and into the evening. In the cities, only a minority of businesses observe the siesta. Although government offices do not officially close at lunchtime, public officials are usually unavailable during the midday hours.

SUPPER   The evening meal usually consists of a combination of boiled roots, with eggs, bread, spaghetti, mashed potatoes, or perhaps *mangu*. Dominicans love sweet desserts, some of which are made from staples such as beans, plantains, and tubers. They candy sweet potatoes and red beans, and make corn puddings. They also enjoy a variety of rich cakes and the pervasive Hispanic caramel custard, flan.

EATING OUT IN SANTO DOMINGO

The country's capital offers a variety of restaurants and international cuisine. In addition to Dominican food, diners have their choice of Italian, French, Chinese, Mexican, and Argentine cuisine, as well as a few vegetarian and fine seafood restaurants.

In the streets, vendors sell snacks of *tostones*, sausages, and *quipes* (KEE-pays), which are fried dumplings filled with meat or cheese. One can also buy fresh juice or sodas, and coffee or espresso.

Snacks are available from street vendors.

FEASTS

While any large gathering might provide an excuse for celebration with food and drink, the most common occasions are Christmas Eve, the New Year, Easter, Carnival, and local patron saint's days. Celebrations usually involve specially prepared Dominican staples such as rice and beans, but might also include meat or fish, and *sancocho*.

EASTER The Easter meal is based on fish, typically fresh or cured codfish, served with potatoes.

CHRISTMAS The main dish of the Dominican Christmas meal is *lechón asado* (lay-CHON ah-SAH-doh), or roasted pig; the younger the pig, the more tender and flavorful. *Lechón asado* is served with rice cooked with beans or pigeon peas. The meal might also include turkey or chicken, and cassava, spaghetti, or fresh green salad. Traditionally, Dominican families raised their own Christmas pig, carefully feeding it all year in

126

PARTY FOOD & ETIQUETTE

There are a few points of etiquette to familiarize foreign guests with the Dominican way of partying. An evening party in the Dominican Republic is typically characterized by merengue music and a lot of dancing, and children are involved in the party rather than sent off to play among themselves.

In keeping with the ethos of relaxation, guests should never arrive early or even punctually; they should come a little later than the invitation time to be sure that they are not the first to arrive. Guests should also eat a snack in the early evening before going to the party because even though Dominicans serve lots of food at their gatherings, they tend to do so around or even after midnight. This is because the usual custom is to eat and leave. Hosts do not want their guests to leave too early so they delay feeding them as long as possible!

Guests can expect to be treated to a variety of tasty dishes, such as roast chicken, rice and beans, and occasionally *sancocho* (san-KOH-choh). *Sancocho* is a meat stew that is served on special occasions. It includes up to seven different types of meat and uses starchy vegetables, such as potatoes, yams, and unripe plantains. *Sancocho* is flavored with fresh coriander, lemon, and spicy chili sauce and is served with white rice.

Since the hosts would want to be with their guests, those who can afford it will often have their parties catered so that the food arrives piping hot. When that is impractical or too expensive, the hostess and her closest female friends or relatives will supervise food preparation and serving.

preparation for the holiday. Another traditional Christmas custom that has declined in recent years is eating boiled chestnuts.

IN THE KITCHEN

As increasing numbers of women seek employment as domestic servants to escape high rates of unemployment, more and more families find it possible to hire domestic help. Many middle- and upper-class families hire at least one maid to help cook, clean, and do laundry. The maid might either live in the house or come to work only during the day.

Dominican kitchens in the cities are usually equipped with modern electric stoves and refrigerators. In contrast, since many rural areas have no electricity, mothers cook the meals in a clay oven called a *fogón* (fo-GOHN), which is heated with a wood fire. These women must also walk to the nearest river or stream to fetch their water, which they ration carefully throughout the day for their cooking and cleaning purposes.

The Mercado Modelo in Santo Domingo is a traditional market housed in a huge two-story structure rather than in the open air. In the front, a sugarcane vendor waits for customers.

MARKETS

There are three types of marketplaces in the Dominican Republic: the traditional open-air market with row upon row of individual vendors in their stalls or with their wares spread out on blankets; the small-town *colmados*, which sell basic supplies; and the modern supermarket with refrigerated meat and well-stocked shelves.

The Mercado Modelo in Santo Domingo is an amplified version of the traditional marketplace. Crowded with close-set stalls displaying goods of astounding abundance and variety, the market offers tambourines, drums, woodcarvings, ceramics, jewelry, leather belts and saddles, wicker, pocketbooks, cigars, sandals, mahogany rocking chairs, tape cassettes of merengue music, T-shirts, and even voodoo products. Vendors on the outer edges of the market sell fresh poultry, pork and goat, as well as a variety of local produce—cassava, plantains, corn, pineapple, passionfruit, papayas, guavas, bananas, carrots, tomatoes, and potatoes.

Dominicans love to bargain over prices and become disappointed or contemptuous if denied the opportunity. The standard procedure begins when the shopper asks, with feigned indifference, the price of a particular product. No matter what price the vendor quotes, the buyer expresses shocked disbelief and a sense of disappointment, then rallies with a lower offer. The vendor reacts to the offer with disgust or dismay and starts to put away the item while throwing out a slightly lower price than originally quoted. The buyer might either give in and pay the lower price or try to pressure the vendor to lower it even more by starting to walk away.

Small-town *colmados* sell basic supplies such as rice, oil, sugar, salt, and rum. A single vendor manages the store, and the goods are generally sold at a fixed price.

Only the larger cities and towns have modern supermarkets, where women from the middle and upper classes do their shopping. The supermarkets exemplify a more modern, but impersonal, convenience.

In the urban areas, women in the lower classes generally shop at the large general marketplace, with its individual vendors, for their finished products such as shoes and clothes. Wealthier women shop for clothes at more expensive, European-style boutiques.

Food is spread out on the ground in an open-air market.

DULCE DE COCO
(COCONUT MILK CREAM)

This recipe makes four servings.

3 cups grated coconut
4 cups evaporated milk
2 cups water
¹/₂ cup sugar
¹/₄ cup raisins
4 cinnamon sticks

Mix all the ingredients in a pot. Boil over low heat, stirring regularly to prevent the mixture from sticking to the pot. When the mixture thickens, turn off the heat. While the mixture is still hot, distribute into small bowls. Leave to cool, then refrigerate for 20 minutes before serving.

MORO DE HABICHUELAS ROJAS (RICE WITH RED BEANS)

This recipe makes four servings.

³/₄ cup washed dried red beans
4 cups water
2 tablespoons olive oil
¹/₂ white onion, diced
2 cloves garlic, ground
¹/₂ green pepper, diced

1 tablespoon tomato paste
1 chicken bullion cube
¹/₂ teaspoon white vinegar
1 ¹/₄ cups rinsed white rice
¹/₂ tablespoon fresh cilantro
¹/₂ tablespoon fresh oregano

Soak the beans overnight. Bring the beans and the water to a boil in a pot, then simmer until the beans are tender. Drain the beans; keep 2 ¹/₄ cups of the water for use later. Heat the oil in a deep pan. Sauté the onion, garlic, and pepper for a few minutes. Add the tomato paste and sauté for a few minutes. Add the beans and sauté for one minute. Add the bullion cube, vinegar, and half of the water. Mix well and cook for 5 minutes. Add the rice, cilantro, oregano, and remaining water. Mix well and cook uncovered on medium heat until the water is almost completely absorbed. Cover with a tight-fitting lid and simmer on very low heat until the rice is tender. Remove from the stove, and leave covered for 5 minutes before serving.

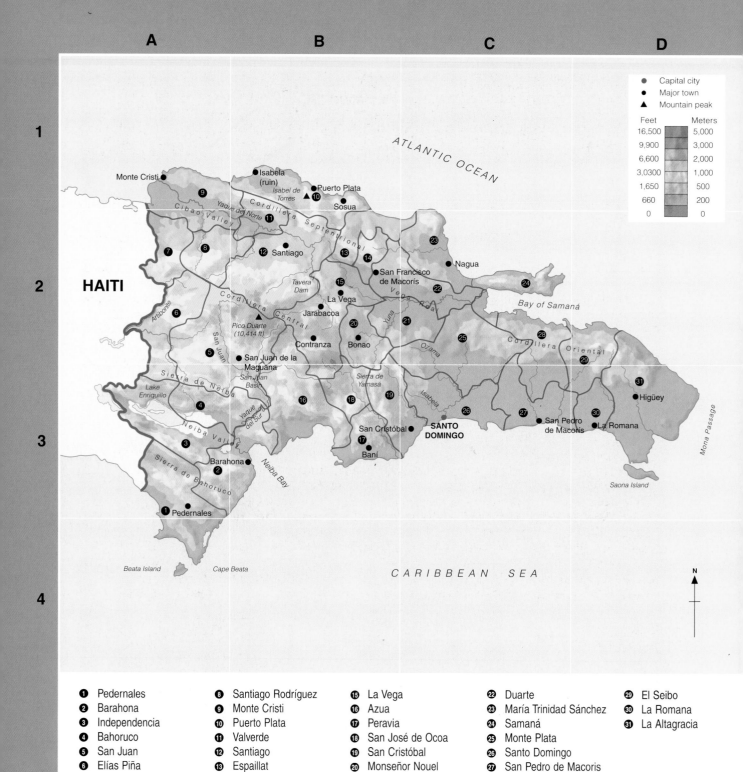

	A	B	C	D

ATLANTIC OCEAN

Legend
- ● Capital city
- ● Major town
- ▲ Mountain peak

Feet		Meters
16,500		5,000
9,900		3,000
6,600		2,000
3,0300		1,000
1,650		500
660		200
0		0

Monte Cristi

Isabela (ruin)

Isabel de Torres ▲ ⑩ Puerto Plata

Sosua

⑨

Cibao Valley

Cordillera Septentrional

Yaque del Norte

⑪

⑦ ⑧ ⑫ Santiago

⑬

⑭ San Francisco de Macorís

㉓

Nagua

HAITI

Cordillera Central

Tavera Dam

⑮

La Vega

㉒

Vega Real

㉔

Bay of Samaná

Artibonite

⑥

Jarabacoa

Pico Duarte (10,414 ft) ▲

Contranza

⑳ Bonao

Yuna

㉑

Ozama

㉕

Cordillera Oriental

㉘

San Juan

⑤

San Juan Basin

● San Juan de la Maguana

Sierra de Neiba

Lake Enriquillo

Neiba Valley

Sierra de Bahoruco

④

Yaque del Sur

⑯

Sierra de Yamasá

⑱

⑲

Isabela

SANTO DOMINGO

San Cristóbal

㉗ San Pedro de Macorís

㉙

㉖

⑰ Peravia

Baní

Barahona

②

③

Neiba Bay

㉚

㉛

● Higüey

La Romana

Mona Passage

① Pedernales

Beata Island   Cape Beata

CARIBBEAN SEA

Saona Island

N

❶ Pedernales	❽ Santiago Rodríguez	⑮ La Vega	㉒ Duarte	㉙ El Seibo
❷ Barahona	❾ Monte Cristi	⑯ Azua	㉓ María Trinidad Sánchez	㉚ La Romana
❸ Independencia	❿ Puerto Plata	⑰ Peravia	㉔ Samaná	㉛ La Altagracia
❹ Bahoruco	⑪ Valverde	⑱ San José de Ocoa	㉕ Monte Plata	
❺ San Juan	⑫ Santiago	⑲ San Cristóbal	㉖ Santo Domingo	
❻ Elías Piña	⑬ Espaillat	⑳ Monseñor Nouel	㉗ San Pedro de Macoris	
❼ Dajabón	⑭ Salcedo	㉑ Sánchez Ramírez	㉘ Hato Mayor	

MAP OF THE DOMINICAN REPUBLIC

ECONOMIC
DOMINICAN REPUBLIC

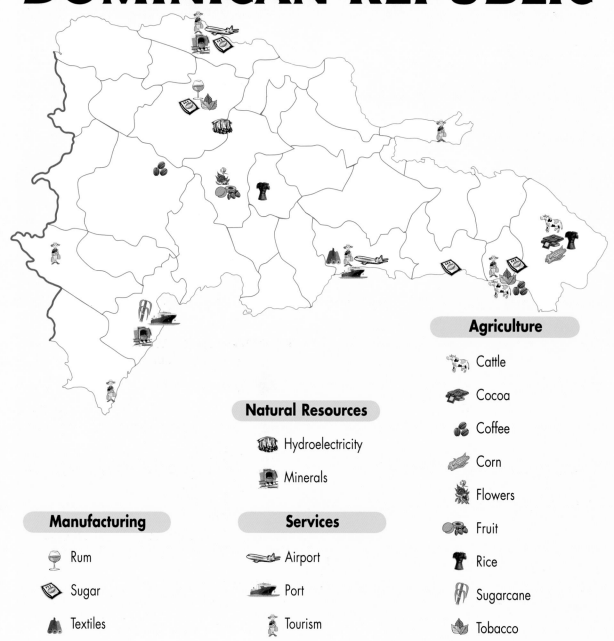

Natural Resources

Hydroelectricity

Minerals

Manufacturing

Rum

Sugar

Textiles

Services

Airport

Port

Tourism

Agriculture

Cattle

Cocoa

Coffee

Corn

Flowers

Fruit

Rice

Sugarcane

Tobacco

ABOUT THE ECONOMY

OVERVIEW
The Dominican economy has been shifting from an agricultural to a service orientation since the 1980s. The country has had some of the highest growth rates in the region, especially in tourism, but Dominicans now have to deal with wide wealth gaps.

GROSS DOMESTIC PRODUCT (GDP)
$52.71 billion (2003 estimate)
Per capita $6,000 (2003 estimate)

GDP BY SECTOR
Agriculture 10.7 percent, industry 31.5 percent, services 57.8 percent (2003)

LAND USE
Arable 22.65 percent, permanent crops 10.33 percent, other 67.02 percent (2001)

NATURAL RESOURCES
Nickel, bauxite, gold, silver

CURRENCY
1 Dominican peso (DOP) = 100 centavos
Notes: 5, 10, 20, 50, 100, 500, and 1000 pesos
Coins: 1, 5, 10, 25, 50 centavos; 1 peso
USD 1 = DOP 26.995 (December 2004)

AGRICULTURAL PRODUCTS
Sugarcane, coffee, cotton, cocoa, tobacco, rice, beans, potatoes, corn, bananas; cattle, dairy products, eggs

INDUSTRIAL PRODUCTS
Sugar processing, ferronickel and gold mining, textiles, cement, tobacco

INFLATION RATE
27.5 percent (2004 estimate)

WORKFORCE
2.3 to 2.6 million (2000 estimate); agriculture 17 percent, industry 24.3 percent, services and government 57.8 percent (1998 estimate)

UNEMPLOYMENT RATE
16.5 percent (2004 estimate)

MAJOR EXPORTS
Ferronickel, sugar, gold, silver, coffee, cocoa, tobacco, meats, consumer goods

MAJOR IMPORTS
Food products, petroleum, cotton and fabrics, chemicals and pharmaceuticals

MAJOR TRADE PARTNERS
United States, Canada, Haiti, Venezuela, Mexico, Colombia (2003)

MAJOR PORTS
Barahona, La Romana, Manzanillo, Puerto Plata, San Pedro de Macorís, Santo Domingo

CULTURAL DOMINICAN REPUBLIC

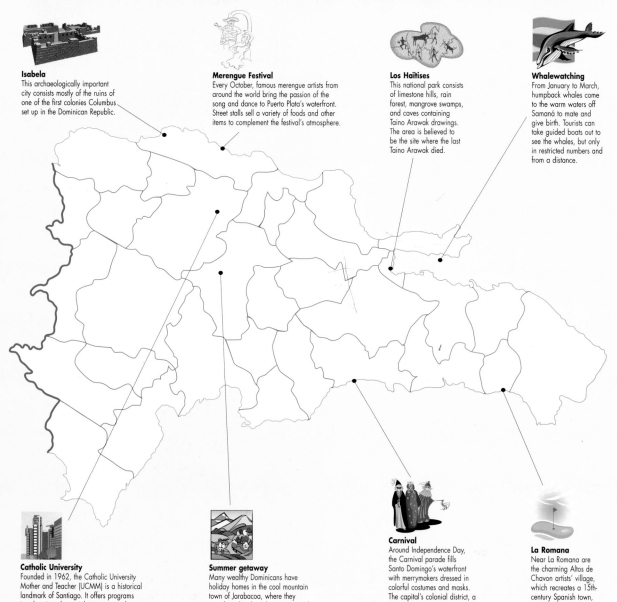

Isabela
This archaeologically important city consists mostly of the ruins of one of the first colonies Columbus set up in the Dominican Republic.

Merengue Festival
Every October, famous merengue artists from around the world bring the passion of the song and dance to Puerto Plata's waterfront. Street stalls sell a variety of foods and other items to complement the festival's atmosphere.

Los Haïtises
This national park consists of limestone hills, rain forest, mangrove swamps, and caves containing Taino Arawak drawings. The area is believed to be the site where the last Taino Arawak died.

Whalewatching
From January to March, humpback whales come to the warm waters off Samaná to mate and give birth. Tourists can take guided boats out to see the whales, but only in restricted numbers and from a distance.

Catholic University
Founded in 1962, the Catholic University Mother and Teacher (UCMM) is a historical landmark of Santiago. It offers programs in education, the social sciences, medicine, engineering, business, and law.

Summer getaway
Many wealthy Dominicans have holiday homes in the cool mountain town of Jarabacoa, where they spend weekends and summers amid pine trees and cherries.

Carnival
Around Independence Day, the Carnival parade fills Santo Domingo's waterfront with merrymakers dressed in colorful costumes and masks. The capital's colonial district, a UNESCO World Heritage Site, exudes new-world charm.

La Romana
Near La Romana are the charming Altos de Chavon artists' village, which recreates a 15th-century Spanish town, and the famous Casa de Campo resort.

ABOUT THE CULTURE

COUNTRY NAME
Dominican Republic

CAPITAL
Santo Domingo

OTHER MAJOR CITIES
Santiago, San Pedro de Macorís, La Romana

GOVERNMENT
Representative democracy

STATE FLAG
Segmented by a white cross into four rectangles, two blue and two red. In the center of the cross is a coat of arms: a shield supported by an olive branch and a palm branch. Above the shield is a blue ribbon with the words *Dios, Patria, Libertad* (God, Fatherland, Liberty), and below the shield is a red ribbon with the country's name.

NATIONAL ANTHEM
Quisqueyanos valientes (*Valient Sons of Quisqueye*)

POPULATION
8.8 million (2004 estimate)

LIFE EXPECTANCY
67.63 years; men 65.98 years, women 69.35 years (2004 estimate)

LITERACY RATE
85 percent

ETHNIC GROUPS
White 16 percent, black 11 percent, mixed 73 percent

RELIGIONS
Roman Catholicism 95 percent, Protestantism and others 5 percent

OFFICIAL LANGUAGE
Spanish

NATIONAL HOLIDAYS
New Year's Day (January 1), Epiphany (January 6), Our Lady of Altagracia (January 21), Duarte's Birthday (January 26), Independence Day (February 27), Carnival (variable), Good Friday (variable), Labor Day (May 1), Corpus Christi (variable), Restoration Day (August 16), Our Lady of Las Mercedes (September 24), Constitution Day (November 6), Christmas Day (December 25)

LEADERS IN POLITICS
Juan Pablo Duarte—liberator (1844)
Rafael Leonidas Trujillo Molina—dictator (1930–61)
Joaquín Balaguer Ricardo—president (1966–78, 1986–96)
Leonel Fernández Reyna—president (1996–2000); reelected in 2004

LEADERS IN THE ARTS
Ramón Oviedo (painter), Manuel de Jesus Galván, (writer), Juan Bosch Gaviño (writer), Héctor Incháustegui Cabral (poet)

TIME LINE

IN THE DOMINICAN REPUBLIC	IN THE WORLD

5000–4000 B.C.
First humans migrate from Central America.

753 B.C.
Rome is founded.

116–17 B.C.
The Roman Empire reaches its greatest extent, under Emperor Trajan (98–17).

A.D. 200
Arawak migrate from the Caribbean.

A.D. 600
Height of Mayan civilization

1000
The Chinese perfect gunpowder and begin to use it in warfare.

1492
Christopher Columbus arrives.

1496
Santo Domingo becomes the first Spanish colony in the Western Hemisphere.

1530
Beginning of trans-Atlantic slave trade organized by the Portuguese in Africa.

1558–1603
Reign of Elizabeth I of England

1620
Pilgrims sail the *Mayflower* to America.

1697
Treaty gives western Hispaniola to France and eastern part to Spain.

1776
U.S. Declaration of Independence

1795
Spain cedes eastern Hispaniola to France.

1789–99
The French Revolution

1808
Spain retakes eastern Hispaniola.

1822
Haitian president Jean-Pierre Boyer annexes eastern Hispaniola.

1844
First Dominican Republic proclaimed

1861
Return to Spanish rule

1861
The U.S. Civil War begins.

1865
Spain withdraws.

1869
The Suez Canal is opened.

1906
Fifty-year treaty with the United States

1914
World War I begins.

IN THE DOMINICAN REPUBLIC	IN THE WORLD
1916–24 U.S. occupation	
1930 General Rafael Leonidas Trujillo Molina establishes dictatorship.	
	1939 World War II begins.
	1945 The United States drops atomic bombs on Hiroshima and Nagasaki.
	1949 The North Atlantic Treaty Organization (NATO) is formed.
1961 Trujillo is assassinated.	**1957** The Russians launch Sputnik.
1962 Juan Bosch becomes president in first free elections in nearly four decades.	
1966 Joaquin Balaguer, Trujillo's designated successor, is elected president.	**1966–69** The Chinese Cultural Revolution
1978–86 The PRD holds the presidency but has to deal with devastating hurricanes in 1979 and riots in 1985 over rising prices.	**1986** Nuclear power disaster at Chernobyl in Ukraine
1986, 1990, 1994 Balaguer is reelected president.	**1991** Break-up of the Soviet Union
1996 Leonel Fernandez Reyna is elected president.	**1997** Hong Kong is returned to China.
1998 Hurricane Georges devastates the republic.	
2000 Hipolito Mejia is elected president.	**2001** Terrorists crash planes in New York, Washington, D.C., and Pennsylvania.
2002 Balaguer dies.	
2003 High prices and power cuts lead to protests.	**2003** War in Iraq
2004 Leonel Fernandez is reelected president.	

GLOSSARY

bateyes (bah-TAY-ays)
Caneworker settlements. Inhumane conditions in these settlements have provoked protests over human rights abuses.

bohíos (boh-EE-ohs)
Huts in which permanent agricultural workers live on company land.

cacique
The chief of a Taino Arawak village.

campesino
A farmer or peasant.

caudillo
A military dictator.

ceiba
The silk cotton tree.

colono (koh-LOH-no)
A small, independent sugarcane grower.

comida criolla (koh-MEE-dah kree-OH-yah)
The name for Dominican cuisine.

compadrazgo (kom-pah-DRAHZ-goh)
A system of godparentage.

dicho (DEE-choh)
A saying or expression.

fucú (foo-KU)
A sign that is likely to bring bad luck.

indigenous
An adjective that describes an ethnic or cultural group as being the original people of a region.

infrastructure
Basic networks and systems necessary for a community to function, such as electricity, water, transportation, and communication.

la novena (la noh-BAY-nah)
Nine consecutive days of prayers.

merengue
A style of music and dance believed to have originated in the Dominican Republic, or Haiti.

minifundios (mee-nee-FOON-dyos)
Small landholdings, the most common form of agricultural holdings in the Dominican Republic.

quinciñera (keen-see-NYAY-rah)
The big 15th birthday celebration of girls from wealthy Dominican families.

tostones (tohs-TOHN-ays)
A popular snack of fried green plantains.

Voodoo
A religion practiced by Haitians in the Dominican Republic. It combines African animist beliefs and Roman Catholic rituals.

yolas (YOH-lahs)
Open boats used by illegal Dominican migrants to Puerto Rico.

FURTHER INFORMATION

BOOKS

Cambeira, Alan. *Azúcar! The Story of Sugar*. Atlanta, GA: Belecam & Associates, Inc., 2001.

Moya Pons, Frank. *The Dominican Republic: A National History*. Princeton, NJ: Markus Wiener Publishers, 1998.

Sosa, Sammy and Marcos Bretón. *Sosa: An Autobiography*. New York: Warner Books, Inc., 2000.

Stratton, Suzanne (editor). *Modern and Contemporary Art in the Dominican Republic*. Seattle, WA: University of Washington Press, 1997.

Wucker, Michele. *Why the Cocks Fight: Dominicans, Haitians, and the Struggle for Hispaniola*. New York: Hill and Wang, 1999.

WEBSITES

BBC News Country Profiles: Dominican Republic.
http://news.bbc.co.uk/1/hi/world/americas/country_profiles/1216926.stm

Central Intelligence Agency World Factbook (select Dominican Republic from the country list).
www.cia.gov/cia/publications/factbook

Dominican Republic News and Travel Information Service. www.dr1.com

Embassy of the Dominican Republic in the United States. www.domrep.org

Library of Congress: Federal Research Division: Country Studies (select Dominican Republic from the country list). http://countrystudies.us

Ramón Oviedo. www.ramonoviedo.com

U.S. Department of State report on human rights in the Dominican Republic.
www.state.gov/g/drl/rls/hrrpt/2004/41758.htm

FILM

Caribbean Close-up: Haiti & the Dominican Republic. Maryknoll World Productions, 1999.

In the Time of the Butterflies. Directed by Mariano Barroso. Metro-Goldwyn-Meyer, 2004.

My American Girls: A Dominican Story. Directed by Aaron Matthews. Filmmakers Library, 2000.

MUSIC

Caribbean Island Music: Songs and Dances of Haiti, the Dominican Republic and Jamaica. Various artists. Nonesuch, 1998.

Colors of the World Explorer: Dominican Republic. Various artists. Allegro Corporation, 2000.

Putumayo Presents: República Dominicana. Various artists. Putumayo World Music, 2000.

The Rough Guide to Merengue and Bachata. Various artists. World Music Network, 2001.

Tierra Lejana. Super Uba. The Orchard, 2003.

BIBLIOGRAPHY

Black, Jan Knippers. *The Dominican Republic: Politics and Development in an Unsovereign State.* Boulder, CO: Westview Press, 1986.

Haggerty, Richard A. *Dominican Republic and Haiti: Country Studies.* Washington, D.C.: Federal Research Division, Library of Congress, 1991.

Haverstock, Nathan A. (editor). *Dominican Republic: In Pictures.* Minneapolis, MN: Lerner Publications, 1988.

Jacobs, Francine and Patrick Collins (illustrator). *The Tainos: The People Who Welcomed Columbus.* New York: G.P. Putnam's Sons, 1992.

Klein, Alan. *Sugarball: The American Game, the Dominican Dream.* New Haven, CT: Yale University Press, 1991.

Mintz, Sidney and Sally Price. *Caribbean Contours.* Baltimore, MC: Johns Hopkins Press, Ltd., 1985.

American Cetacean Society Humpback Whale Fact Sheet. www.acsonline.org/factpack/humpback.htm

CIA World Factbook: Dominican Republic. www.cia.gov/cia/publications/factbook/geos/dr.html

FAO Country Profiles and Mapping Information System. www.fao.org/countryprofiles

Humpback Whale Behavior Maui Hawaii. www.whalewatchmaui.com/behavior.html

Organization for Economic Cooperation and Development. www.oecd.org

World Bank Group. www.worldbank.org

World Gazetteer. www.world-gazetteer.com

INDEX